RETIREMENT

AND

OTHER MYTHS

Musings on the Leisurely Life with a Dash of Humor & Advice

ELLIOTT RICHMAN

R&E Publishers
Saratoga, California

R & E Publishers
P.O. Box 2008, Saratoga, CA 95070
Tel: (408) 866-6303   Fax: (408) 866-0825

Book Design by Diane Parker

Library of Congress Card Catalog Number: 93-43072

ISBN 1-56875-074-9

CONTENTS

INTRODUCTION

Expressing thoughts and feelings in prose has been difficult at times. Mixing recollections, experiences, and observations in rhyme has been a joy. I recall reading Ogden Nash poems to my young daughters, rather than typical nursery rhymes. They may not have understood them, but they fell asleep, while I provided myself with constant enjoyment. This collection is not intended to emulate his work in any way, except in spirit. If you are retired, laugh with me. If you are not, here's a taste of what you may be in for. Other targets of my musings should strike home with people watchers of all ages.

ELLIOTT RICHMAN
SARASOTA, FL.

RETIREMENT

"VOLUNTARY" RETIREMENT

In days gone by, they used to say
    If you want to enjoy each year
You mustn't drink or eat too much
    and NEVER volunteer

But rules do change when you retire
    and move to a sunnier clime
You may eat and drink as you see fit
    Relax, and have a good time

Up north the economy was based upon
    paying for services, cheap or dear
Down south almost anywhere you go
    You're served by a volunteer

Library, school, sports arena or museum
    Whether side door, front or rear
They couldn't thrive, or stay alive
    without the Volunteer

We start our careers at salaries low
    and strive for wealth and seniority
Then we succeed, and finally retire
    and work all day for charity

You finish school and college too
    To help you make your mark
and then you find you spend your time
    calling strikes at the Little League park

At lunch martinis were the rule
    I've now switched to wine or beer
Instead of selling stocks and bonds
    I'm an unpaid Volunteer

YOU ASKED FOR IT!

Retirement seemed so far away
    I felt I had just been hired
But time, like sex, is too soon gone
    And here I am, retired.

From nine to five I used to toil
    And wished I could be free
And now I'm home around the clock
    Is this where I wanted to be?

My wife who kept our house so well
    Is just as perplexed, you see
Her freedom has been imposed upon
    What does she do with me?

I never cooked a meal or baked
    a cake or boiled a chowder
But now I offer free cooking advise
    As my wife's complaints get louder

"Go play some golf", she wearily says
    Her patience grows ever thinner.
"Enjoy the game, enjoy your friends
    and don't come home till dinner"

"I have a plan", I said one day
    "to make our retirement smoother.
"You take up golf, I'll cook the meals
    and no-one will be the loser"

My wife said "Fine, I'll take up golf
    and with my full permission"
You stay home, enjoy yourself
    I leave you in charge of the kitchen"

She's not only playing golf, it seems
    She also made many new friends
And never spends much time at home
    That's how this story ends.

THE HOBBY LOBBY

For years we spent each waking hour
    on a hobby that wasn't funny
It replaced most other activities
    That hobby was earning money

When you retire, that pressure is off
    and other priorities take hold
We seem to revert to our childhood ways
    If I may be so bold

When you were a tot, for birthdays you got
    electric trains to run
In retirement leisure, you again take pleasure
    playing model railroad for fun

When our furniture showed signs of age
    We'd replace it with something new
Retirees are avid antique collectors
    like us, the "older the better" is true

Old bottles, dishes and pottery
    We couldn't give away enough
Now we travel to every flea market
    and buy back the same old stuff.

Antique autos appeal to many
    To make them like new is the object
They cost more by far, than a brand new car
    What a money consuming project

My hobbies are more down-to-earth
    I, too, collect odds and ends
Not stamps, or coins, or furniture
    Just debts, pleasant memories, and friends.

TALKING ABOUT WALKING

In our working days we used to get
    all the exercise we needed
In daily life, through toil and strife
    calisthenics went unheeded

Today, alas, as time has passed
    our normal life is quiet
No more do we have a family
    making every day a riot

If you want to stay fit, you must exercise
    the experts all agree
Especially now, they do avow
    if you're over sixty three

I used to jog, morning and night
    no matter what the weather
Five miles each day, rain or shine
    and wore out much shoe leather

Now they say, that's not the way
    to keep your body fit
Just walk and walk and walk some more
    and don't give up or quit

In retirement town, look up and down
    You'll see them all parading
On streets, in parks, and on the beach
    from dawn till sun starts fading

Grandma and grandpa walk each day
    for miles and miles, no less
Not just in plain walking clothes
    but in every sort of dress

Jogging suits in colors bright
    their outfit nothing lacks
It seems that walking must include
    the latest styles from Saks.

Continued

Take big strides and swing those arms
　　to keep the circulation flowing
In our dreams, we're back in our teens
　　and muscles are still growing

Earmuffs are worn in northern climes
　　to protect your ears from cold
We must now wear "Walkman" radio earphones
　　to hear the beat, I'm told.

Alas, alack, when we get back
　　to where we started walking
we find that we, are apt to be
　　the breakfast table stalking.

The calories we just walked off
　　are back on, to our sorrow.
But do not fear, the plan is clear
　　We'll walk twice as far tomorrow.

IT'S "TIME" TO RETIRE

You've worked many years for one corporation
    and finally earned a four week vacation
and into some project you're ready to dive
    You wake up one day and you're 65

The company rules say you must now retire
    Your replacement they're ready to hire
Although you still are hale and hearty
    You now have to face a retirement party

For weeks they've been planning a big affair
    They even want your family all to be there
If you peek you will see them as they collect
    money for your gift, they've yet to select

"What would he like?", they ask your wife
    "What will he enjoy in his leisurely life?"
"I really don't know", she said modestly
    "He really hasn't confided in me"

The party night finally rolled around
    A present they must have surely found
To everyone there, I do beseech
    Please don't ask me to give a speech

At the head table I sat next to the boss
    At compliments he was not at a loss
He never used to give me such praise
    whenever I thought I deserved a raise

The speeches went on and on and on
    through the soup, salad, and filet mignon
One thing I feel is worthy of mention
    None of the crowd was paying attention

They envied me all the fun in store
    The fishing, golf, tennis, and more
I hoped that the gift might be
    golf clubs or a fishing outfit for me

They finally came to the final speech
    and said I was lucky retirement to reach
My leisure they toasted with a glasses of scotch
    and then gave me a lousy wrist watch!

THE "SNOW BIRD" INVASION

I used to be a "snow bird"
    Which means that yearly we
would leave our icy northern home
    and drive south merrily

We always thought it wonderful
    to thaw our freezing bones
The snow and grind we left behind
    to get those sun tanned tones

Now we've moved to Florida
    No more commuting for our crowd
We'll stay right here, throughout the year
    where snow and sleet are not allowed

Once you've moved to the sun belt
    Your attitude seems to change
Though I used to be a "Snow Bird"
    Now I wish they'd stay home on the range

In summer we have little traffic
    The restaurants are nearly empty
The golf course is ours to enjoy
    and parking spots are a'plenty

Then winter comes, and we must face
    the big "Snow Bird" invasion
Like locusts they fill up every space
    All sorts of cain they're raisin'

We wait in line almost all the time
    For services we once took for granted
The restaurants are bursting at the seams
    and prices are "Snow Bird" slanted

But what about the "Sun Birds"?
    Who live here all year round
The loyal few who pay their way
    when no "Snow Birds" can be found

We used to think of the Fourth of July
    as a wonderful holiday
but now we look forward to Easter time
    That's when "Snow Birds" go away

MORNING MEDIA MANIA

I used to read only the morning headlines
    Featuring accidents, politics, and crime
Then rush to work without another look
    For details, I had no time

When I came home, the news was old
    so the paper was discarded
But first I took one quick look
    at when the football game started

Now I'm retired, and have more time
    to read each word they print
At the crack of dawn, I stifle a yawn
    and down the driveway I sprint

What's new today, I eagerly say
    as I open the local journal
I can hardly wait to read the fate
    of criminals infernal

Next I turn to the business page
    to learn who's been acquired
It's nice to be out of the old rat race
    with no chance to be fired

Financial offers catch my eye
    Good investments   abound
What good is maturity in twenty years
    I doubt that I'll be around

The sports pages are the next I see
    Who lost and who managed to win
I agree with those who always say
    The "designated hitter" is a sin

The local news I then peruse
    with mixed feelings, mostly of hate
The political air will curl your hair
    I feel I'm living in a "Third World" state

Continued

Then the weather page I find
    Will it rain and for how long?
As long as they use percentages
    the forecasters can't be wrong

For years the comic pages went
    unnoticed in my life
Now I must sally through Gasoline Alley
    and keep up with Dagwood's wife

The advertisements fill each page
    "Too Much!" I want to shout
In spite of that, you can bet your hat
    I cut all the coupons out

The Editorial page is best of all
    Each column is important to see
I must admit, I have a fit
    When they don't agree with me.

Obituaries must be scanned
    To find out who's still alive
and then I save each wrinkled page
    To give to the paper drive

ADULT EDUCATION

Kindergarten, Grammar school, High school, and college
    We spent many years acquiring much knowledge
Yet after retirement, we rush out the door
    to adult classes, it seems we want more

Despite all the prior schools we attended
    "Keep your mind busy" is highly recommended
Forget all your know how, that life you're leaving
    It's now painting, sculpture, and, yes, basket weaving

If I start mixing drinks in our cocktail glasses
    "Forget it" my wife shouts, "We're late for our classes"
What am I supposed to do with all this new lore?
    It has raised havoc with my golf score!

NOW HEAR THIS!

We enjoy the local jazz concerts
    Great numbers from the forties and before
To really "dig" that music
    You must be sixty or more

Radio stations call them "Golden Oldies"
    or so I had been told
I listened for an hour or so
    and became completely "rocked and rolled"

You must be growing older
    if you still think Sinatra's sublime
but the thing that really dates you is
    Elvis Presley is "after" your time!

Ella, Sarah, Dinah Washington too
    could make any tune sound sublime
As I listen to the new breed of singers, I fear
    my tastes are "before" their time.

Monday used to be, a miserable day for me
    as I groaned the "back-to-work" song"
Since I've retired, in pleasure I'm mired
    My weekends are seven days long.

Twinge in the back, crick in the neck
    Aches and pains that fright us
After you reach a ripe old age
    you can blame it all on arthrit-us.

You can always tell, when you don't feel well
    (Remember this little moral)
The flu you've got, when your body is hot
    Be it rectal or be it oral

A trip to the opthomologist
    was something I never desired
Until I missed the fine print, and took the hint
    Eyeglasses are now required

I don't really think it's very fair
    to have your face lifted on Medicare!

My desk was always organized and neat
    At efficiency I was the best
Now that I have finally retired
    my desk is a storage chest.

I try to rest my head on my comfortable bed
    but I toss and turn instead
Best of all is the sleep I get
    on my chair in front of the TV set

As we recycle more and more
    to help with the environment
I'd like to recycle the years before
    I started my retirement

I drink a toast, and proudly boast
    of my achievements in days of yore
My friends all groan, and run for home
    They've heard it ten times before.

We had grippe, and croup, and sniffles
    But today there's something new
No matter what your symptoms
    You've got some type of Flu.

I went to my high school reunion
  We laughed at all our old jokes
After a while, I lost my smile
  Do I look as old as those folks?

Most days are alike when you retire
  The weeks seem to go by much quicker
The way I tell when Sunday rolls around
  The newspaper is much thicker.

At most restaurants and movie theaters
  Senior discounts make a hit
What really makes you feel twice as old
  is to get one without asking for it

I find it hard to ignore
  people I've met once before
But I'm no good at playing the game
  of trying to remember their name

I used to think, quick as a wink
  whenever a problem arose
Now I pause, and clench my jaws
  That comes with age, I suppose

When your joints are racked with pain
  it's easy to blame it on the rain
If it hasn't rained, I'm forced to say
  Your arthritis is probably here to stay.

Sunday morning used to be the time
    to linger in bed and nuzzle.
As time passes, you reach for your glasses
    and nuzzle with the crossword puzzle.

I thought that upon retirement
    Rest and relaxation would be my environment
But I'm so busy, on foot and by car
    I have no time for R and R

It's hard to recall, in summer or fall
    that winter is colder and horrider
But as for me, no snow will I see
    I've decided to stay in Florid-er

We had our company's retirees reunion
    Full of good cheer and tall tales
No wonder everyone looked so relaxed
    No more worry about next month's sales!

It's hard to remember, the snows of December
    The sleet, and the slush, and the ice
Those winters before, I choose to ignore
    We're now in the sun belt, how nice!

The morning paper is full of bad news
    Robbery, murder, dumb political views
That's why, when my morning coffee I guzzle
    I quickly turn to the crossword puzzle

Nobody likes to grow older
    That's why I really get sore
when I hear Maurice Chevalier sing:
    "I'm glad I'm not young anymore"

Doctors, oh doctors, heed my call
    Who are your favorite patients of all?
"That's easy" they answered to a man
    "Those with the best insurance plan"

I took a chance, and agreed to dance
    to rock music at a local affair
When I held my partner in the old-fashioned way
    they all turned around to stare

Pain relievers fill each store
    They never run out, there's always more
Medicine ads crowd each newspaper page
    Forget them, pain comes with old age.

You may not be as sharp as you were
    Old age may be partly to blame
As for me, my memory works real well
    I'll never forget "What's his name"

I could give you a lot of sage advice
    on success, and what it takes
But, no, I'll keep it to myself
    Like me, make your own mistakes

Good-bye Summer, hello Fall
    For most, their vacation has passed
To me it matters not at all
    I'm retired and the whole year's a blast

We tend to forget, the older we get
    that tastes change with each generation
The new music and clothes, cause me to propose
    They're awful, but not worth the aggravation.

Young drivers are in such a great hurry
    swerving madly from left lane to right
I always derive great satisfaction
    When they're stuck with me at the next light

Yesterday I should have cut the grass
    Instead I chose fishing for some bass
Today I awoke lazy, to my sorrow
    If my luck holds out, it'll rain tomorrow

For all the years before I retired
    my job I never did shirk
Weekday crowds now fill ballparks and beach
    Doesn't anyone go to work?

A calendar works almost like a gear
    It's stuck in "forward" from year to year
Time flies so fast, it couldn't be worse
    If only we could shift it into "reverse"!

I spend a good many waking hours
    pruning shrubs and trimming flowers
It's an established fact, as each barber knows
    The more you cut, the faster it grows.

They flock to the sunbelt to escape the cold
    Never again a snow shovel to hold
But as soon as hot summertime arrives
    they rush back up north like bees to their hives.

Every so often, I throw out my back
    for many days in pain I wrack
It really throws me into a rage
    when friends all say: "It comes with age"

THE CYCLE CYCLE

As soon as children learn how to walk
    Sometimes before they know how to talk
We give them a tricycle of their very own
    to pedal around until they have grown
in a few years, their legs are stronger
    and this "baby's" bike will do no longer
Then comes a two-wheeler with training wheels
    which makes them feel like such big deals
Eventually, the training period passes
    and they race on two wheels to their classes
In later years, as they grow in size
    there are 10-speed racers for real exercise
Finally comes old age, arthritis, and then
    Grandma's back on a tricycle again!

A birthday is an event to enjoy
    until you've reached fifty-nine
When your sixties have begun, it's not as much fun
    You don't improve with age, like wine.

When you don't feel well, it's hard to tell
    if it's something you ate, or your age is too great.

I'm sure you've seen those garage sales
    attended by both husband and wife
You might call all that junk assembled
    the "waste basket" of their life.

As you mature and as time passes
    you rely more and more on your eyeglasses
Many mornings, you may panic and fright
    if you forget where you put them last night.

WHINING
AND
DINING

THE EARLY BIRD

We used to eat at a fashionable hour
    Or whenever our hunger stirred
But now we dine at a crazy time
    To catch the "Early Bird"

A restaurant is a place where we
    would relax and enjoy the decor
Instead we gulp our lunch at ten
    since the Early Bird starts at four

By now you'd think we should have learned
    to do our own cooking, broiling, and baking
But somehow once you have retired
    Most dinners out you'll be taking

Spacious homes and Condos too
    are designed for us to live in
but tell me wife, if we eat out all our life
    Why did we buy a kitchen?

In my business life, my lonely wife
    complained: "You never eat at home"
And now she finds, daily kinds
    of reasons for us to roam.

Just when I feel, this night's ideal
    for an evening of TV football
Without a doubt, we must rush out
    To beat the crowd at the mall

The experts say, you should each day
    eat three meals, in the south or the north
But if we make the "Early Bird"
    I'm hungry for a fourth.

It's funny how your outlooks change
    As you get old and gray
Instead of "How's the stock market range?"
    It's "Where do we eat today?"

THE DIET RIOT

Fashion magazines get on my nerves
    Those models are so painfully thin
Experts state, we're all overweight
    The problem is, where to begin?

Giving up sweets, and fatty meats
    We know is the smart thing to do
We tried all that, and still we're fat
    It's time to attempt something new.

Jane Fonda made a new video
    guaranteed to take off inches
Night and day, we did it her way
    Alas, our belt still pinches!

Let's try those advertised diets
    Special milk shakes for lunch and dinner
How can this food, which tastes so good
    be used to make you thinner?

If you drink too many diet shakes
    You'll gain a few more pounds
Why didn't we follow instructions?
    "Two a day", the label expounds.

We jogged and walked and exercised
    Till we couldn't stand the pace
But after stepping on the scales
    All that we lost was "face".

I guess we're fated to be heavy
    Really, what's so wrong with that?
Fashion models may be skinny
    But it's more fun to be fat.

SPICE IS THE VARIETY OF LIFE

What ever happened to dinner at home?
  These days, after six, we all seem to roam
To ethnic restaurants scattered far and wide
  Which one to choose can be tough to decide

Food is available from each foreign shore
  If you like variety, there couldn't be more
Yet sometimes I'd like a rest from this pace
  and stop forcing that strange food in my face

Chinese dining has become a big thing
  I doubt if you'll find this food in Beijing
I carefully choose from the large bill-of-fare
  but an unwritten law says you always must share
My meal was carefully chosen without any haste
  Why must I eat to someone else's taste?

If French cuisine is what you choose
  be prepared for a lot of money to lose
The menu in French is quite a mystery
  I should have studied French, not History
Portions are small, in sauce they are drowned
  So what? Think of the wine you have downed

Italians are known for the food that they eat
  I hope you like pasta, they don't serve much meat
Pepperoni, and cheese, and red sauce are a must
  It's like eating pizza without the crust
After all that macaroni and spaghetti
  We go home to recover. Believe me, I'm ready

There are many other ethnic places to eat
  We've tried them all, searching for a treat:
Indian cafes I avoid in a hurry
  It takes three days to forget the curry
Thai food is easy to find
  Chinese food with explosives, it'll blow your mind

Continued

I like Greek dances, and their moussaka too
    but goat cheese and grape leaves, I'll leave for you
Mexican restaurants are not what they claim
    To be perfectly truthful, "Tex-Mex" is their name
If you specialize in Spanish food, it would be nice
    to serve something other than black beans and rice

Next week we're going to try someplace brand new
    An African eatery that features roast Gnu.

WHAT'S COOKING?

The fine art of cooking is an enigma to me
    The thumbs on my left hand count up to three
Often I feel that I made a mistake
    not learning to fry, or to broil, or to bake
Many of my friends not only enjoy it
    Their wives relax and let them employ it.
It's very strange to hear them harangue
    about how much egg white goes in a meringue.
Or how they time their dough to rise
    to make a perfect crust for their pies.
From time to time, I've tried my hand
    but everything tasted too salty or bland.
The toughest of all, is not knowing whether
    all of the food will be ready together.
Pictures on frozen food packages look nice
    but when I try one, the middle's still ice.
Microwaves are replacing the old kitchen range
    It's fast all right, but the food's color looks strange
Even my barbecue cannot be sold
    The steaks are all burned and the hamburgers cold.
I'm fortunate my wife is the best of cooks
    without even a glance at her many cook books
Our dining arrangements have worked out just fine
    I love her meals, and she can't stand mine.

Don't eat candy, turn down that drink
    My liver says "That's the way"
But the liver's a weaker organ
    and my stomach rules the day.

———————————

Most dogs and cats eat very well
    with meals devised by veterinarians
After watching those pet food commercials
    We decided to be vegetarians.

———————————

A meal is not considered complete
    without a salad on the side
I'll eat tomatoes, lettuce and such.
    It's broccoli I can't abide.

———————————

Martinis are not the only way
    to feel the effect of liquor.
Beer or wine may calm you down
    but gin works a whole lot quicker.

———————————

"Fast food" is an American staple
    It attracts most people's eye.
Does "fast" mean the way you eat it?
    Or the speed at which I drive by?

———————————

Sugar-free food and low-fat milk
    are good for your health, I hear.
I'll buy that, if it cuts your fat.
    But why, oh why, "light" beer?

———————————

Never trust a restaurant
    where there's always immediate seating
You may have lots of space, in that empty place
    The crowds have gone where there's good eating.

———————————

Doughnuts are great, the day that you buy 'em
　　They taste like a bagel, if too late you try 'em

I tried to like pizza, our new national food
　　but to me, a hot dog tastes twice as good
Furthermore, I'm usually neat as a pin
　　and pizza always drips down my chin

It remains a big mystery to me
　　as to what in French restaurants people see
"Petit" is the size of the portions they serve.
　　and the bill would strain the Federal Reserve

A bottle of wine, when you're out to dine
　　has become the "in" thing to drink
The fruit of the vine may be very fine
　　but I'll stick to martinis, I think.

A "Dumbwaiter" was a contraption
　　to bring up the soup and the meat
There still are many dumbwaiters today
　　but they're running around on two feet.

If you're a sea food lover
　　doesn't it make you squirm
whenever you eat a scaly fish
　　that likes to eat a worm?

I watch my diet throughout each meal
　　Then at the dessert menu I peek
No matter how much I fight it
　　out comes the "chocolate freak"

As a morning "pick-me-upper"
    fresh coffee is the best for me
If I drink coffee after dinner
    it's a "keep-me-upper" until three

We love to entertain at home
    To our friends go our best wishes
We'd value their friendship even more
    if they'd help us wash the dishes

Here's a warning, oh friend of mine
    The next time you go out to dine
and you're tempted to order a fine bottle of wine
    Be prepared for the size of the check you'll sign.

Ocean cruises are claimed to be
    the vacation that everyone wants
If you ever take one, you will see
    they're just floating restaurants.

Fast food restaurants have grown like weeds
    serving Junk food that nobody needs
If you really want greasy food, there's no place finer
    than the good old-fashioned neighborhood diner

It seems every restaurant now has a salad bar
    To eat like a rabbit, you needn't go far
I wondered after I made my trip
    Since I served myself, who gets the tip?

Dinner theaters are popular places
    for a meal and a show in the same night
If the play is good, your food gets cold
    If it's bad, there goes your appetite!

Why do we eat at "fast" food places ?
    Why should dining be a day at the races?
As for me, I'd much rather go
    where good food is served, and the eating is slow.

It used to be simple to order a soft drink
    You Just stepped up and asked for a "Coke"
Now there are "light", "caffeine free", "diet" and more
    To call them "Cokes" is a joke!

If you would like to start a riot
    tell a rancher meat is bad for your diet.
To instigate a very angry mutter
    advise a dairyman you've given up butter.

How do you choose a good restaurant?
    Some seek the ambiance or a view
Don't depend on the tastes of a friend
    and a critic's review just won't do

All that's left is to try your luck
    and guess which are good or bad
Sometimes for dinner, you can pick out a winner
    but a good many times, you'll be "had"!

Don't ask me why, but I had to try
    a Japanese Sushi bar
Their most popular dish, seemed to be raw fish
    That's going a little too far!

Here's good advice you'd better heed
    Suppress your desire, stifle that greed
as that yummy dessert menu you read
    Chocolate cream pie is the last thing you need.

Microwave ovens are here to stay
    If you're in a hurry, there's no faster way
It zaps frozen food, how really incredible
    Ignore the fact that it never looks edible.

———————

When we eat at a Chinese restaurant
    I choose carefully from the bill-of-fare
but for some unexplained reason
    I must share it with everyone there.

ANIMAL CRACKERS

A "PET" COMPLAINT

There is an old expression
    that once was widely known
That life begins when your pet expires
    and your children have all left home

So why do so many old couples
    who've retired and are finally free
to come and go as they see fit
    come home with a new puppy?

And there are all those others
    who's working days have ended
who can't wait to add to their household
    a cat which must be tended

We're free at last to have a blast
    and travel the whole world round
But wait, we can't depart just yet
    A good kennel must be found

With your grey hair, the Medicare
    will help with the doctor's bills
But even in a welfare state
    You must pay for your animal's ills

Your neighborhood, it looks so good
    The lawns and streets are super
In order to comply with the local laws
    You must carry a "pooper-scooper"

As a lawyer once, you used to work
    with plaintiff and defendant
Now you're retired, and have been hired
    as your dog's bathroom attendant.

VIEW FROM THE ZOO

Nature in the wild is preferable to
    seeing animals caged in a zoo
Since we can't travel abroad in our quest
    You have to settle for second best

Some zoos give animals room to roam
    trying to simulate their natural home
It does give us all a chance to see
    a large variety, although they're not free

Monkeys always seem to be at play
    Apes and gorillas never act that way
With each other, they constantly fuss
    No wonder it is said they're related to us

Lions and tigers pace constantly up and back
    I'm sure it's not food that they lack
Maybe the exercise is what they need
    No, they probably wish they were freed

The elephant, a large stately beast
    They eat quite a lot, to say the least
In Africa, grass and leaves fill their frame
    Here they beg for peanuts, ain't it a shame?

In most zoos, there are kangaroos
    From Australia is where they have sprung
We must admire their anatomy
    with a pocket to carry their young

The rhinoceros is a blunderbuss who
    can knock over most of his foes
Be careful if he smells you out
    There's a sharp horn on top of his nose

Never trust a hippopotamus
    While in the water he will lazily loll
He may be a vegetarian, but
    his big mouth could swallow you whole

Continued

Deer of all types lazily graze
    For beauty it's hard to beat 'em
The reason they enjoy their life in the zoo
    Nobody's trying to eat 'em

A camel is really a dromedary
    His shape is quite extra-ordinary
It's easy a camel to straddle
    His humps form a built-in saddle

I love to see a peacock strut his stuff
    But sometimes that's not quite enough
When he really wants a female to quail
    He opens up his fabulous tail

A giraffe always makes me laugh
    as he looks down at me in disdain
I wonder if aspirin is any help
    when that long, long neck has a pain.

Zebras look like a genetic mistake
    that a careless horse breeder might make
Why pen them in, my stars!
    They already are behind bars.

Why do they call them "laughing"?
    Hyenas really look very blue
Maybe they all stop smiling
    when they're locked up in a zoo

Polar bears look so uncomfortable
    as they lie in the heat near their moat
Too bad Mother Nature didn't
    put a zipper on their fur coat

Seals are everyone's favorite
    as they glide through the water and squawk
As swimmers they're very graceful
    but not when they try to walk

Continued

There are so many other animals
　　I marvel at their variety and scope
While zoos are interesting for people
　　The free beasts will thrive, I hope.

WITH APOLOGIES TO AUDUBON

I once thought that watchers of birds
　　were people closely allied to nerds
Now that I have seen bird's splendor
　　Deepest apologies I hereby render

Unlike humans, where women display color
　　Male birds are dressy, females are duller
People go to extremes just for idle dating
　　Birds preen and prance only for serious mating

As a beginner, the trouble I find
　　is I see many birds, but I don't know what kind
I madly flip pages of my new bird book
　　but most fly away before a good look

Although I'm new at this bird watching game
　　There are quite a few that I can now name:

Pelicans look so awkward on land
　　As dive bombers, they can be quite grand
Sea gulls are found on every beach
　　Keep your picnic out of their reach
Have you ever seen a giant blue heron?
　　It looks like a feather toupee he's wearin'
Snowy white egrets patiently wait
　　If a fish comes too close, it will be ate
Anhingas are cousins to the cormorant
　　Electric feather dryers they really want

Continued

Cardinals wear uniforms of bright red
    All except for their pointed head
Large winged hawks are very graceful
    When prey is spotted, he soon gets a faceful
America's symbol, the eagle is called
    With a head full of feathers, why call him bald?
The woodpeckers a mystery to me
    What a headache he must get from every tree!
Whenever you see pigeons, I must tell you that
    I wouldn't walk under them without a hat
A robin's diet can make you squirm
    It's O.K. to eat berries, but never a worm!
Most birds are calm and seldom worry
    sandpipers are always in a big hurry
Black Birds are another species to know
    but how do you tell a raven from a crow?
I've watched the antics of the sandhill crane
    Their mating dance is impossible to explain
Why does everyone think the owl is so wise?
    They look pretty dumb with those big staring 'eyes
Life for chickens is very dim
    We eat her eggs, and then we eat him
Turkeys seem to lead a very healthy life
    Yet most end up going under the knife.

There are many other bird types and classes
    you can only see well with spy glasses
But if of the great outdoors you are wary
    You'll have to settle for a parakeet or canary

RAISING KIDS IS FOR THE BIRDS

Have you ever watched birds building a nest?
>From dawn to dusk they toil at their quest
for grass, straw, and twigs and then place them just so
>so the nest will be safe when strong winds blow.
They finally finish, with no time to spare
>without further delay, the eggs are all there
They take turns hatching the eggs in the nest
>one goes for food, while the other will rest.
Before very long, the chicks appear
>Beaks wide open, hungry peeps you can hear
>From morn to night both parents try
>to fill the stomachs of their small fry
The bigger they get, the more they eat.
>Soon they're flapping and hopping on both feet
Then one day, they all fly away
>The nest is empty, and I must say
Birds have it easy, their young have departed.
>With humans, parental problems have barely started.
It takes many more years to empty our nest
>through high school, and college, and all of the rest!
And it must be said, even after they've wed
>they're back in our "nest" often, so they can be fed
It's still not over, but next comes real fun
>The grandchildren visit, one by one
While birds may keep busy, nesting in mangers
>all of their offspring are total strangers.

Ducklings always make me smile
　　as they swim behind mama, single file
Like all other youngsters, they soon mature
　　and try to avoid being roasted, to be sure.

―――――――

I finally know, though it's taken me a while
　　the difference between an alligator and a crocodile
If you see either one, in Florida or the Nile
　　Don't get too close, they'll cramp your style.

―――――――

A squirrel kept falling to the ground
　　and I heard him mutter these words:
"No matter what other squirrels have found,
　　making love in a tree is for the birds!"

―――――――

A spider is an expert engineer
　　spinning its web from there to here
A curious fly, moth, or even a gnat
　　will get wrapped up and eaten in nothing flat.

―――――――

I'll let you in on a little secret
　　How to tell a heron from an egret
One is white, the other is gray
　　or could it be the other way?

―――――――

We went to the famous Sea World
　　and watched the dolphins at play
If they could watch us play our brutal games
　　I wonder what they would say?

―――――――

If there's a snake in our back yard
　　we immediately start to run
It's hard to tell, when you're scared as hell
　　if its after you, or just enjoying the sun

How do you train a new puppy
    to stop messing under the bed?
If only we could teach him
    the newspaper's not there to be read!

I sit at my window and watch the birds
    flying from tree to tree
I'm not an expert, so I can't tell
    the he-birds from the shes.

In Florida's tropical weather
    Egrets carefully preen each feather
I find it hard to imagine that
    they once killed them to decorate a hat.

The amazing thing about a heron
    is how long it can stand perfectly still
It doesn't move a feather, no matter the weather
    But, boy, is it fast on a kill!

Every alligator that I see
    makes quite an impression on me
Don't move too close for a better view
    He can make quite an impression "in" you.

Most dogs wag their tails and play
    any time of the night or day
Ain't it a shame we can't do the same
    instead of grouching our life away.

A Wild West show, called a rodeo
    is not meant to make you laugh
But all the while, I have to smile
    at huge cowboys wrestling a tiny calf

I sometimes feel like a prig
　　when I turn up my nose at a pig
These animals nobody really loves
　　yet we eat them, and wear them as gloves.

――――――――

Chickens seem to spend all day
　　pecking, and pecking, and pecking away
I hate to think of, what they eat and drink of
　　especially when they're on my dinner tray.

――――――――

I looked down at a gator swimming by
　　and bravely looked him in the eye
He returned my stare with a hungry glare
　　I'm glad I'm up here and he's down there!

――――――――

I watched a small lizard on a plant
　　poised to attack each bug and each ant
It seems such patience is a waste
　　He obviously doesn't have a gourmet taste

BATTERIES
NOT INCLUDED

COMPUTER GAMES

Computers are a wondrous advance
    Each scientist proclaims
Too bad this marvel of our age
    is wasted on silly games

Silicon chips and discs and bytes
    With these you can't go wrong
With all of this I have to ask
    Why use it for "Donkey Kong?"

In school and home we proudly state
    Computers can be run by first graders
With all this training I regret to say
    They use it for "Space Invaders"

Instead of making bold new strides
    in understanding science and the sun
Our younger folk, with a masterful stroke
    can "zap" with a laser gun

I recall that once our engineers
    worked with slide rules, logic, and care
and games were played on a playing field
    and the games didn't curl your hair

What good is a baseball game where you
    can't touch the ball or bat?
and computer golf is nothing like
    The feel of where it's at

So let's get back to playing games
    where games are supposed to be played
and use our computers for progress
    and not for an "alien raid"

It's not just that I'm growing old
    and can't work the "joystick" with ease
I like things in their proper place
    So back to the ball field, please.

THE POWER THAT BE

I tried one day to make a list
    (I'm sure there are some things that I missed)
of items electric on which we depend
    It went on and on almost without end.

The kitchen seemed a good place to start
    Oven, microwave, refrigerator were only part
of the army of appliances I did meet
    soaking up power so we can eat.

We have to stay clean, so let's make room
    for dish and clothes washers, and the vacuum
It's not quite done if it's still wet
    so hair and clothes dryers complete the set

Home entertainment also depends
    on how much power the utility sends
Stereo, radios, VCR and TV
    Add the computer to this category

Each electric light had to be counted
    Then telephones, both desk and wall-mounted
Can't forget air conditioning and heat
    plus electric blankets to warm our feet

The garage included many more
    power tools like the electric saw
How about all the electric fans?
    and openers for garage door and aluminum cans.

I gave up after my list consisted
    of fifteen pages of items I'd listed
You may take this with a grain of salt
    but if the power fails, our life would halt!

THE TELEPHONE REVOLUTION

Alexander Graham Bell had an idea
    Use a wire to hold a conversation
For that it worked well, till progress befell
    It's no longer just station-to station

We phoned Grandma to wish her well
    even made calls to other nations
Now other things use these same telephone lines
    from FAX to airline reservations

New gimmicks abound, more daily are found
    to complicate this simple invention
"call waiting" is here, but one thing is clear
    "waiting" was not Bell's intention!

Answering machines are the latest device
    which many attach to their phone
If I have an important message for you
    Why must I wait for the "tone"?

For the life of me, I do not see
    why portable phones are now used
If you cannot call from a phone on the wall
    your life must be very confused

When I need repairs, or covers for our chairs
    I want to shop and compare
Instead of bargaining, I'm besieged by telemarketing
    Please, I only buy when I'm there!

Oh yes, now you find, phones of every kind
    The old fashioned phone is no more
You can buy any type, any color you like
    hidden dials, crazy shapes galore

When I learned to drive, to help stay alive
    I was told "keep both hands on the wheel"
Now it's no use, car phones are profuse
    No wonder more danger I feel.

Continued

Information operators used to help
   when you needed a number or advice
Now there's a change, I find it strange
   to talk to a computer device.

With all these "improvements" now in place
   May I suggest something better?
I would not jest, give your phone a rest
   Hang it up and write them a letter!

NO SALE !

Even if you possess an average brain
   TV commercials should make you complain
Instead of encouraging me to buy them
   they have convinced me never to try them
I use my car to get me from home to work
   not to speed around mountain roads like a jerk
I occasionally drink beer to quench my thirst
   not because at wild parties girls choose me first
When my stomach acts up on me
   the last thing I need is a cure on TV
Perfume is a product they sell and they sell
   Why would you buy some without even a smell?
Record album commercials are tuneful and gripping
   The real rip-off is "Handling and Shipping"
Each airline claims they're the best in the nation
   Reaching them by phone is a major frustration
Talk about a "pig-in-a-poke"
   Buying insurance by phone is really a joke
The TV Home Shopping Network sells everything on earth
   as long as you don't mind paying twice what it's worth
If you really want to put your finances in danger
   Phone your credit card number to a TV stranger
A final word of advice, before I go
   Do your shopping in person, not on a TV show!

The computer's a clever invention
    It's choice of options is complete
If only in life's troubled waters
    We could push a button and "delete".

My VCR, the handbook reads
    performs in a magical way
How come every time I set the hour
    I forget to punch in the day?

I taped a TV program
    To watch when my time was more free.
After I blipped out the commercials
    There was nothing much left to see.

Personal computers have caused quite a flap
    but why would you want to hold one in your lap?

The VCR is an interesting product
    for a moderate rental fee
you can stay home and watch movies
    you never, ever wanted to see.

When you buy a new appliance
    the warranty "can't be beat"
but keep it too long, and they sing the same song:
    "This product is now obsolete"

Television is not what it used to be
    Today the announcers proudly proclaim:
"We reluctantly interrupt our commercials
    to bring you what's left of the game"

To illustrate how bad TV programs can grow
    Commercials have become more entertaining than the show

If you mess with your stereo system
    to remove a part to be fixed
You'd better remember where all the wires go
    or, like me, you'll end up between and betwixt

We prefer watching movies on our VCR
    They can be viewed evening or morn
When you turn it off, you're right at home
    and you don't have to eat popcorn.

You don't need a high school course in science
    to purchase an electrical appliance
But the lack of knowledge makes you feel like a jerk
    when you plug it in and can't get it to work.

A telephone is a remarkable device
    For talking to grandchildren it serves very nice
But lately I find more time spent on the phone
    asking salesmen to leave me alone

My computer arrived, fully equipped
    More pieces than I expected were shipped
Would someone please explain to me
    what a "Joystick" is supposed to be?

In this overdone electronic age
    there's a law I'd like to see
(Before our brains go completely dead)
    A ban on daytime TV

My ego is shattered, I must confess
    The computer always defeats me at chess

Today's students will probably get ahead
    That is, if their calculator batteries don't go dead

Television is heavy with advertising
    The agencies try hard to be cute
Hats off to whoever invented
    that wonderful button called "mute"

If you want to be left alone
    buy a device that will answer your phone
I, however, always feel like a creep
    talking to a machine, "after the beep"

A computer is a smart electronic device
    that I found easy to procure
It never seems to really trust me
    and keeps popping up with "Are you sure?"

If I were to list all the movies we've missed
    it would take me from now to next fall
But now with our new VCR in place
    good or bad, we're seeing them all.

GET THE MESSAGE?

Communicating is getting expensive
    especially if it must be extensive
The government holds us hostage
    by annually raising the postage
Despite the "Long distance company of your choice"
    it costs plenty to transmit your voice
You can now FAX for good measure
    That bill will raise the blood pressure
My thoughts are not really reportable
    about car phones and those that are portable
I would like to stop communicating
    To most, that would be devastating
My solution to this dilemma, perhaps somewhat mean
    is to not answer my answering machine
I quickly erased the messages that arrived every day
    The need for me to communicate soon faded away
As a result, I lost all my business and friends
    and that is how this story ends!

POLITICAL
FOLLIES

S-ELECTION DAYS

"Primary" is supposed to mean "First of All"
    New Hampshire traditionally gets that call.
It seems that by the time they're all finished
    the primary importance of primaries is diminished.
My suggestion is impossible, some may say
    "Why not all primaries on the same day?"
Finally, this expensive nonsense is completed.
    We still don't know who won, and who were defeated.
I'm firmly convinced it is their intention
    to keep us in suspense until the convention.
So we must sit and wait for many months more
    before we determine who to vote for.
For weeks before the convention takes place
    the ballyhoo exceeds the Indy 500 race.
Newspapers and TV use this occasion
    to divert our attention from our vacation.
Finally the time of the convention arrives
    Delegates swarm into town like bees into hives.
Covered with buttons, decked out in silly hats.
    Not like the old days of derbies and spats.
From all around the nation, with spirits hearty
    resembling a crowd at a masquerade party.
Speakers drone on, it seems without end.
    Nobody's listening, they're each talking to a friend.
The party's platform, important, you think?
    It's quickly adopted, back to food and drink!
Nobody knows what's going on in their minds.
    All you can see are hands waving a sea of signs.
High on the platform, speeches seem to bore
    but TV interviews dominate the floor
They finally arrive at the issue at hand
    Who do they propose to rule this land?
Despite the forecasts and all the surmises
    you quickly discover there'll be no surprises.
The favorite sons don't stand a chance
    The candidate has been selected well in advance.

Continued

The delegate's high point is finally here.
    Endless parades, and cheer after cheer.
It's sad to think, upon reflection
    To go through all this for candidate selection.
If you work for the party, they probably say
    You can go to the convention and party and play.
The rest of us now have the chore
    of deciding who's the best, and what is more
We have to choose who we are buying
    Who's telling the truth, and who is lying.
Unfortunately, we have a national tradition
    that forces us to vote for a politician!

WHITE HOUSE FOLLIES

I can recall many presidents
    in the years that I've been around
Each was entirely different
    At least that is what I have found

Herbert Hoover was the first
    He wore a starched white collar
As an engineer he was very smart
    but the bottom fell out of his dollar.

F.D.R. promised to save us
    since we all were down on all fours
After he designed the welfare state
    we won the war "to end all wars"

Then came Harry Truman
    Not too popular at first, I fear
But after a while, he showed his style
    and proved "The buck stops here"

Ike did a]ob on the enemy mob
    and was drafted to serve us all
As far as I can tell, he did real well
    particularly with his golf ball

Continued

John Kennedy brought in a new look
    of youth and art and laughter
His life was shortened tragically
    but other Kennedys keep coming after

Lyndon Johnson roared into town
    with the Texas flag a'flying
He spent our money in foreign lands
    At home, Lady-Bird did the buying

Like a work of fiction, was Richard Nixon
    Always serious, and very haughty
In China he was a real hero
    But in Watergate he was naughty.

We then picked Jimmy Carter
    His Georgia gang could do no harm
Jimmy never had so many problems
    at home on his peanut farm

What can you say about Ron Reagan?
    He "acted" with charm and good cheer
Don't worry about fiscal problems
    Relax, cause the Gipper is here.

George Bush was the next leader
    They called him a "wimp", that's right
Who needs oil for electrical power
    Just plug in the "thousand points of light"

I don't mean to sound sarcastic
    My hat's off to all that mob
We should all be very thankful
    that anyone would want such a job.

If you want a civics lesson
    Don't watch Congress in session.

IRS forms come in the mail
    at the very start of the year.
It seems such a long time till April 15th
    but in the blink of an eye, it's here.

I watch the Ethics Hearings
    on C-SPAN all day long
They spend an awful lot of time
    to prove no-one did anything wrong.

Young people now have the right to vote
    the Supreme Court did expound
In some strange way, on Election Day
    These new voters cannot be found.

A Lobby is an entrance to a theater
    or office or public building
In politics it's a pressure group
    I'd say more but the lily I'd be gilding.

The British Parliament is very loud
    They all shout when the speaker's mistaken
Our Congress is much quieter
    Since most of their seats are not taken.

Don't ever think you've got it made
    when all your monthly bills are paid.
I warn you that you can't relax
    Have you forgotten the income tax?

The Congress seems to be in hysterics
    now that they've rediscovered ethics.

I heard an optimistic speech by an economist
    There must be something that I missed
Economic forecasts would take a new twist
    if those experts would price our food shopping list!

Politicians as a whole
    don't seem to have a specific goal
With public opinion they seem to roll
    When in doubt, they take a poll.

Televising Congress in action is here
    But don't you find it very queer?
As they orate on subjects too numerous to mention
    None of their peers pay any attention

When I try to understand the wording
    in an advertised zoning change
I throw up my hands in frustration
    I guess that's what the lawyer's arrange.

We remember many great Americans
    Their accomplishments we all hail
Isn't it a shame that George Washington
    is honored with a department store sale?

As I watch our congressmen at work
    At giving long speeches they never shirk
As they leave each session in single file
    their brains remain on "their side of the aisle"

Our Board of County Commissioners
    according to what I have read
hire outsiders to solve all their problems
    Why not elect those consultants instead?

If you're looking for a disillusion-ment
    watch congressmen in their confusion-ment
Senators do not perform any stronger
    It's just that their terms are longer.

Daily papers I eagerly peruse
    TV anchormen give me their views
The world situation is a lighted fuse
    All this news gives me the blues

I wrote our local council a letter
    to tell the County how to do better
at spending our hard-earned tax
    But they weren't interested in facts.

Secret documents are marked "Confidential"
    To see them, government clearance is essential
"Confidential" for movie stars seems to mean
    you can read it in a supermarket magazine

If we had the campaign money politicians spend
    all our deficit problems would come to an end

The "Mid-East" is a hotbed of different cultures
    all after the spoils, like flocks of vultures
In the U.S.A., I've heard by word of mouth
    it's the same with congressmen from the "Mid-South"

Despite much study and serious reflection
    I face a quandary at each election
There isn't a candidate I want to come in first
    and find myself choosing the "best of the worst"

––––––––––––

Party platforms at both national conventions
    are loaded with promises and good intentions
The candidates forget them once they're elected
    Memory is an attribute they have seriously neglected

WEATHER OR NOT

Space stations and moon probes are common today
    We're exploring the universe in every which way
Scientists' achievements astound one and all
    Yet they still can't tell us if rain will fall
At NASA, 100% accuracy is what they must use
    Still we get "20% chance of rain" on the TV news
I suspect they are protecting their reputation
    by not sticking their necks out re precipitation
They are 100% accurate, I hasten to say
    about what sort of weather we had yesterday

WINNER TAKES A FALL

We used to produce the best steel, cars, and such
    When I remember it, my heart quickens.
Alas, we have lost our manufacturing expertise
    That is, except for all those chickens.
Our production base is losing the race
    to Germany and the Far East
To save our face, we still hold first place
    in fast food and hamburgers, at least.
If we can make guns, and ships,
    and planes and sophisticated missiles in space

Continued

For the life of me, I fail to see
    why we're losing the peacetime race.
But have no fear, the day draws near
    when we will reign once more
When we run out of money, things will turn sunny
    We'll recover with another war.
But this time we'll choose, not to win but to lose
    and as a result of this defeat
The victors will rebuild us, as we did for them
    and then we'll be back on our feet.

NEXT TIME, PRESIDENT CLINTON

I read that your first Cabinet was tough to choose
    Next time take this advice, what can you lose?
To insure the Attorney General will not be voted down
    I recommend nominating Murphy Brown
Your Treasury Secretary, Bentson, seems quite a frump
    To handle the money, why not Donald Trump?
The Secretary of State must be tactful and sedate
    John McEnroe could easily fill that slate
The Labor Secretary has jobs to protect
    The Yankee's George Steinbrenner will be correct
The Agriculture Secretary is in charge of what we eat
    Julia Childs would fix everyone a treat
The Drug Czar must be quite tough
    How about Noriega? He knows that stuff.
For Secretary of Defense, how's this plan?
    The football Giants Lawrence Taylor, he's the man!
Secretary of Transportation, a tough one to pick
    Lee Iococca would do the trick
The Press Secretary should be in the know
    If you can believe him, then choose Perot!
If you again choose Al Gore to be your Vice
    A Dale Carnegie course would suit him just nice
These appointments may not be your favorite seatings
    but they'll sure liven up the cabinet meeting.

THE LANGUAGE
BARRIER

WHO'S CONFUSED?

If a "bough" is a branch of a tree
    and a "beaux" you love tenderly
Wait, a "bow" is something you tie
    No, a "bow" causes arrows to fly.

"Slight" is a multi-purpose word
    it describes a small amount
"Slight" could also mean a snub
    "Slight" of hand you must also count.

Your scale measures what you "weigh"
    Miss Muffet ate her curds and "whey"
This language confuses me
    in a strange and mysterious "way".

If you're in the will you're called an "heir"
    The poetic form of before is "ere"
Some people refer to Ireland as "Eire"
    I think I'll stop and get some "air"

A "fete" is a celebration
    You walk on both your "feet"
It's a "feat" to win a contest
    If you don't you'll go down in de-"feat"

If that's not enough of this silly stuff
    try "meet" and "meat" and "mete"
You'll be pleased to "hear", I'll stop right "here"
    It is "sweet" to end this "suite".

YOU DON'T SAY

Many of the expressions we use every day
    to me don't really mean what they say
So you won't be put in awkward positions
    I'll give you some literal definitions:

"Hot Stuff" - Too much Mexican food
"Dead Right" - Turn left, if you're shrewd

"Top Dog" - The best tasting wiener
"Make Tracks" - Then call the rug cleaner

"Right On" - Now try the left shoe
"Sad Sack" - Your dress makes me blue

"It's A Gas" - Something to do with digestion
"What's Up?" - A very personal question

"Can Do" - A visit to the john
"Old Hat" - If it fits, put it on

"No Way" - A dead end street
"Dead End" - Too long on a hard seat

"Watch Out" - Can't tell time of day
"Far Fetched" - Dragged a long way

"Leave Off" - In Autumn they fall
"Flat Tire" - No air left at all

"No Go" - Ugh, you stay
"Easy Street" - Downhill, I'd say

"Red Herring" - A communist fish
"Have A Blast" - Could be a death wish

"No Dice" - We can't shoot craps
"Glad Rags" - Happy wearing scraps?

"Dumb Luck" - A three leaf clover
"No Fair" - The carnival's over

Continued

"Holy Cow" - Her udder has burst
"Fail Safe" - Thrown out at first

"Bottom's Up" - Teenagers mooning
"Pipe Down" - The plumbing you're ruining

"Top Notch" - A crease in the head
"Break A Leg" - Can he mean what he said?

"I'm Beat" - The complaint of a drum
"How Come?" - I hitchhiked with my thumb

"Take Heart" - Better call a surgeon
"Better Fish To Fry" - Salmon or sturgeon?

"Fire Sale" - How much for a flame?
"Fair Play" - The umpire's to blame

"Come Clean" - Take a bath at home
"Stay Put" - No more will I roam

"Fat Chance" - If you eat all day
"Fat Free" - They give it away

"Drop In" - Come take a fall
"Due Bill" - Aren't they all?

"Kickback" - I guess with your heels
"Driving Range" - The stove is on wheels

"Go-Between" - I hope there's room
"Hell's Bells" - They toll your doom

"Dead Right" - Go left to survive
"Quick Stop" - A bad way to drive

"French Fried" - Pierre's drunk again
"Woman's Lib" - No freedom for men

"Venetian Blind" - Gondolier in trouble
"Eye Sore" - I'm seeing double

"Monkey Business" - Dealing with zoos
"Rye Bread" - The baker used booze

Continued

"Cold Turkey" - The ice show's a flop
"Hot Dog" - His sweating won't stop

"De-Frost" - De ice on de ground
"In-Law" - where attorneys are found

"Lay-Off" - I guess I've been fired
"Get Lost" - No more verses, I'm tired!

FICTION-al DICTION-ary

re-TIRING:	New wheels for your car
de-GRADING:	The worst mark, by far
STAG-nation:	You can't find a date
de-PRESS-ion:	Your suit's wrinkled state
be-LIEV- ing:	I think you should go
be-TRAY- ing:	The waiter's too slow
ex-TENDED:	The baby sitter left
ex-PEN-ded:	The inkwell's bereft
de-LIBERATE:	We can't let you out
DEMON-strate:	A devil, no doubt
dis-GUST-ing:	Turning off the fan
de-BATING:	The fish ate and ran
INCUM-BENT:	My salary is twisted
de-MEANING:	In the dictionary is listed
dis-COVER:	The bedroom's too hot
re-COVER:	Our furniture is shot
ex-AMPLE:	We've run out of room
pre-AMBLE:	I'll walk pretty soon
DELI-cious:	Corn beef on rye
PRETEN-tious:	You're only nine, don't lie
de-LIVER-ing:	From too much to drink
de-SIGNING:	Disappearing ink

Continued

VACAT- ion:	You're out on the street
ex-PULS-ion:	My heart missed a beat
CONTENT-ious:	Satisfied you're not
no-TORI-ous:	Labor party's my spot
DEPART-ment:	It's time to go home
de-RANGE-ment:	Where antelopes roam
de-VOT-ion:	No ballot is cast
de-TENTION:	The pressure won't last
de-LIGHT-ful:	You've put on more weight
di-STRESS-ful:	It's something I ate
de-FER-ment:	Skinning a bear
de-FACE-ment:	Shaving off your hair

SAY "WHAT"?

What does "Mud in your eye" have to do with drinking?
    Does "Scratch your head" really improve thinking?
Not "Worth a dime" doesn't account for inflation
    Don't "Butt in" defies literal translation
To "Raise the roof" requires a large crane
    "Cats and dogs" don't go out in the rain
"Bottoms up", if you stand on your head
    "Break a leg" will land you in bed
If we "Drop the subject", how far will it fall?
    "No matter what", a mass question, that's all
An "Open house" is difficult to heat
    A "Sweet tooth", you'd better not eat
True "Puppy love" involves wagging your tail
    Don't "Paint the town" or you'll have to raise bail
"Step on it" there's a bug on the floor
    "Flat broke" won't hold air anymore
"Time out" they won't let me come in
    "Tight scrape" is hard on your skin
"No way" you can't get there from here
    "Hit or miss" the choice is quite clear
"Hot shot", my drink needs some ice.
    "Sour grapes" don't taste too nice
"Dead eye" doesn't see very far
    "Fall guy" can't stand up at the bar
"Dead right", living left is my choice
    "Dumb luck" is to win without voice
"Cut it out" that coupon's worth money
    "Short change", your Bermudas look funny
"Home free", no rent to pay
    "Come clean", if dirty, stay away
"Stop gap", your zipper's undone
    "Fat chance", you'll soon weigh a ton
"Lame duck", the birds leg is broken
    "Free ride", no need for a token
"Shape up", straighten your hat
    "Lay off", I'm finished, that's that!

WHAT'S IN A NAME?

I must assume in days of yore
    Your family was named for it's work or trade
Alas, today that is no longer true
    Here are some names where no sense is made:

A tailor is paid to both patch and sew
    Elizabeth and Robert that trade do not know
A miller will grind your corn or grain
    Milling is a job Ann or Arthur can't explain
A cooper makes barrels and repairs them too
    which Gary or Fenimore wouldn't know how to do
Gardeners cut grass and prune each stem
    Ava and Erle have others do it for them
Carters drive people to and fro
    Jimmy and Nell take taxis wherever they go
Players are pianos or pros in a game
    Gary is one whose trade matches his name
A porter carries your bags right along
    Cole carries a tune and writes quite a song
Bakers baked bread, which all of us ate
    James didn't have to bake, he was Secretary of State
Farmers grow food, at which they are handy
    Fannie only knows how to make candy
If you were an archer, you'd own bow and arrow
    George plays golf on fairways quite narrow
A roper, I assume, lassos bulls and calfs
    Elmo takes surveys, and puts them on graphs
A cook prepares meals, both night and day
    Captain explores, and Barbara's in a play
A hunter is expert at killing game
    Tab is an actor, a soft drink uses his name
Brewers are known for their ale and their beer
    Teresa doesn't drink, she sings loud and clear

It's too bad this change has been made
    Nobody seems to follow their ancestor's trade.

YOU "CAN" HAVE IT BOTH WAYS

When you inked the "deed" on your new home
    Did you know you were signing a palindrome?
You may be coming and going, I do believe
    at high "noon", or on saturday "eve"
My car is a "dud", and what is worse
    I can't get the "rotor" to go in reverse
When you stand on the "poop" deck when at sea
    what "level" is that supposed to be?
You may politely "refer" to "mom" as "madam"
    but "dad" was called "pop" ever since adam
If you sneak a "peep" at the fairest of "sexes"
    She may bruise your "eye", or the solar plexus
Babies eat "pap", so does our "pup"
    They constantly "poop", or else they throw up
Backward or forward, palindromes read the same
    Just in case "ewe" "did" want me to explain.

OXYMORONS

Oxymoron is a word not quite fair
    It sound like an idiot full of hot air
Whether it is used in fact or in fiction
    it's meant to imply a silly contradiction
We're all guilty of it from time to time
    You may even find some in this rhyme.
How can a person be "clearly confused"?
    Or, better yet, what is "old news"?
Why do they call them "student teachers"?
    Are "holy wars" started by preachers?
"Pretty ugly" is a hard one to call
    Are "Jumbo shrimp" large or small?
Did Shakespeare really mean "sweet sorrow"?
    Does "open secret" mean you'll hear it tomorrow?
"Fail safe" is not truth, but is fiction
    A "fast stop" if the brakes still have friction
A "fine mess" this has gotten me in
    I need "nothing more" than a shot of "dry gin".

CAUGHT IN THE DRAFT

A "draft" is a rush of cool air
    A "draft" means your book's not quite there
A "draft" could land you in the service
    "Overdraft" at the bank makes me nervous
"Draft" horses pull trucks far and near
    so we can enjoy "drafts" of beer
There are so many meanings of "draft"
    English is an art, not a craft!

SHARP FLATS

A "flat" English folk call their home
    "Flat" beer has lost all it's foam
You may sleep "flat" on your back
    "Flat" tire means get out the jack
If you sing off-key, you are "flat"
    "Flat"-out is your speed round the track
"Flat"-footed is caught in the "ack"!

YOU CAN'T HABIT BOTH WAYS

A "Habit" is clothing you might wear
    Bad "Habits" seem to be everywhere
Whether it be a hare or even a rabbit
    Multiplication is their favorite "habit"!

"UGH", THERE'S THE RUB

At the risk of sounding heretic
    Why isn't English more phonetic?
To make my point, here are samples
    of some un-phonetic examples:
If your throat is sore, you may "cough"
    "Ugh" is what cough should leave off.
When finished, you should be "thru"
    There's an "ogh" with nothing to do
Another "ugh" makes me "laugh"
    Why not cut "laugh" almost in half?
A "thorough" study of words has a purpose.
    You guessed it, "ugh" is again "thoroughly" surplus.
And take "thought", and "caught", and "brought"
    Why is "ugh" in so many words we are "taut"?

Some things I just don't understand
    in our language of such variety
If "high" means you have imbibed too much
    are drunkards in "High Society"?

"Up" in arms, "Down" in the mouth
    water on the "Side", you're the "Tops".
I find after much reflection
    Our language goes in every direction.

"Permanent" is a word that means
    forever or longer I guess
Why do they use it for hairdos?
    And don't believe "permanent" press.

If a word is sought I always thought
    the dictionary could be used
But if I don't know it, what page will show it?
    It's gotten me quite confused.

There are strange New England accents
    and Brooklyn-ese causes a fuss
As a northerner I often wonder
    Do southerners understand us?

———————

A woman's "pocketbook" sounds to me
    like something that she reads.
It actually has turned out to be
    a container for all her needs.

———————

I'm an avid crossword puzzle fan
    I know orcas, anele, and gnus
I wonder why I fill my head
    with words I will never use

———————

"Self serving" is an expression that means
    you do things to benefit you
"Self Service" is a benefit for someone else
    The gas station owner, that's who!

———————

It really helps your vocabulary
    to do crossword puzzles at home
A "Madam" can be either good or bad
    but she's still a Palindrome.

———————

A "single" can be a dollar bill
    or a base hit when you reach first
A "singles bar" is something else
    that has little to do with thirst.

———————

Our official language is English
    but I must this opportunity seize
Law schools have created a second tongue
    Now there's English and "Legalese"

I figured out what "contingency" means
    when you sue someone after a fall
If you lose, it means you get nothing
    If you win, the lawyer takes all!

———————

Needles grow on a pine tree
    Needles are used to knit socks for me
Doctors use needles to inject a shot
    In Needles, California, it's much too hot.

———————

You may cook your dinner in a pot
    On your stomach, a pot looks not so hot
In poker, the pot means a lot
    For this rhyme, I deserve a pot-shot.

———————

To shoot at a bear is not fair
    It's almost too much to bear
If your cupboard is bare, don't despair
    Your bearing is in need of repair

———————

If you're a prude, it's rude to be nude
    A dude may brood over his food
I must allude to our family feud
    You're very crude, if you dare to intrude.

———————

The sweat did pour, out of every pore
    I tore out the door, to go forth to the store
I bought what I wore, on the fourth floor
    Don't get sore, there's no more in store.

———————

It's never really expected
    when with true love you are infected
that the girl you have selected
    will leave you feeling rejected
It's nothing you have neglected
    Don't feel so dejected
It's time that you detected
    with someone else she's connected!

Many things fade into antiquity
    like Atlantis beneath the deep seas
Many words have also faded from sight
    such as: "Thank you", "You're welcome", and "Please"

"Come on down", and "Hurry up"
    are contradictions we often make
While "Quiet down", and "Pick-me-up"
    are the result of prescriptions you take.

Is it a dolphin or a porpoise?
    Is it a turtle or a tortoise?
Is it a rabbit or a hare?
    Is it a grizzly or a bear?
They may each have a distinctive name
    but, to me, they look the same

I'm sorry to tell you: "You're quite a bore"
    Always bragging of "Days of yore"
I wonder what you accomplished last week
    I suspect it was nothing, "so to speak"

You may call it a parasol
    To me it's just an umbrella
On a sunny day, it shades our cones
    Your chocolate and my vanella.

Bracelets are the newest style
    on your ankle in addition to your wrist
Seat belts are worn across your lap
    Your "seat" is completely missed.

A measuring "cup" helps in cooking
    A tea "cup" will hold your drink
A Loving "Cup" is something you win
    For what kind of contest, do you think?

"New" York, "New" Jersey, "New" England
    are new world names, I am told
Whenever I pay them a visit
    they really do look quite "old".

A "spade" is a type of shovel
    In cards, a "spade" is a suit
"Spayed" has the same pronunciation
    It keeps pets from bearing fruit.

Etcetera is a very useful word
    if you want to shorten a list
I can't help thinking when I read it
    there's something important that I missed.

"Mother of pearl" is no relation
    to a great singer named Bailey
"Sob sister" is not a sad relative
    She writes gossip columns daily

Foam sprays, water spouts
    Waves break with much wrath
No, I'm not swimming in the surf
    I'm just giving my dog a bath.

SPORTS SHORTS

HELLO SPORTS FANS

There are many sports to watch on TV
    But the games are not all that you see
Dugouts and bullpens the cameras invade
    plus the partisan fans and half-time parades
Baseball players, they spit and they chew
    It's not a place to walk barefoot through
In plain view, underwear they're adjusting
    If you're a prude, it could be disgusting
The camera constantly turns to the stands
    Up with the wave, chop down with the hands
Linen stores must have a good trade
    selling bed sheets on which all those signs are made
I have a question, if it's not out of place
    Does it help the team when the fans paint their face?
Rich men - poor men, gourmets or not
    Cold hot dogs, warm beer appeal to the lot
Football is played on turf artificial
    The injuries are real, not just superficial
If they really want to extend their career
    install air bags in with the rest of their gear
College football fans couldn't be merrier
    It's like a case of mass hysterier
Their mascots are varied: Tiger, goat or mule
    Do these students spend any time in school?
Good sportsmanship disappeared into air that's thin
    It's not how they play, as long as they win
If you are a coach, and your team won't improve
    Go home and start packing, you'll soon have to move
In basketball games, they push, punch and run
    I call it "foul" playing, if you'll pardon the pun
They collide with full force, the ref doesn't scowl
    But brush someone's finger, oops that's a foul!
Hockey's so fast, to follow it takes luck
    The trouble for me is I can't see the puck
To solve this dilemma, I have a bright notion
    Play back the tape in very slow motion
The fans in the stands never seem to complain
    They sit there through heat, cold, sleet, and rain
That kind of bug hasn't bitten me yet
    I'll stick to the sofa and my TV set.

ANYONE FOR GOLF?

Golf was known when we were young
    As a pastime for the rich
The average person could not play
    Until they had made their niche

Today we find, a different kind
    of golfer on the green
From far away, they rush to play
    whether eighty or thirteen

You needn't own a limousine
    or be chairman of the board
Just grab some clubs, and pay the fee
    which most can now afford

Golf courses abound, the country round
    whether public, semi, or private
You see crowds play, most every day
    regardless of the climate

Golf is a sport that takes much skill
    or so the professional thinks
It's obvious that so many of us
    really don't belong on the links

Fat and thin, short and tall
    They all line up at the tee
For goodness sake, give us a break
    I've been waiting since half past three

Head down, stomach in
    Don't lose your concentration
It would be nice, to heed this advice
    But I'm too old for new education

Another trend, that will not end
    are ladies playing golf daily
"Don't expect me home, you eat alone"
    they tell their husbands gaily

Continued

In golf they use a handicap
    to set the betting prices
But I find that my "handicaps"
    are duffs, and scuffs, and slices

In track they use a handicap
    as you bet which horse will come in first
In golf the handicap just proves
    Who's bad, and who's the worst

When I retired, I promised myself
    to go golfing every day
I'd practice my swing, and my putting
    and really improve my play

Alas, I found that did not work
    As I golf in the blinding heat
The fairways are longer, my body's no stronger
    and I regularly go down in defeat!

TIME FOR A CHANGE

Baseball is still the American game
    The best are enshrined in their Hall of Fame
Far be it for me to rock the boat
    but some changes in rules may be worthy of note.

If eating pumpkin seeds is not what they're doing
    then a gigantic cud of tobacco they're chewing
Can't we stop them from constantly spitting
    and why, oh why, have designated hitting?
If these personal bad habits they care to see
    they should make a tape and watch TV
So many night games, to me it's not fair
    After 4 or 5 innings, I'm asleep in my chair
Pitchers used to throw for nine innings each game
    Now if they last six, it's the Hall of Fame
Stop calling them "bullpens", if the rule allows
    Relievers usually pitch more like "cows"
Sign language was meant for the deaf to advance
    Must third base coaches do the St. Vitus dance?
Another new custom I can't quite understand
    Why do batters wear a glove on each hand?
Baseball announcers talk on till they bore
    Hey, once in a while, why not give us the score?
Oh yes, the computers spit out statistics galore
    Who cares what they did ten years before?
Fans used to keep careful scores on each line
    Now they paint their faces and hang out a sign
Commercials, oh well, I suppose they're necessary
    They make my "mute" button a real necessity
A large TV screen adorns each dome
    If it was TV I wanted, I'd stay at home
Artificial turf may save on lawn mowing
    but multiple fractures seem to be growing
Even fans have changed, be it Pirates or Braves
    Is it all that beer that causes those "waves"?

Don't get me wrong, in spite of it all
    There's nothing to compare with our game of baseball.

SPORTS TALK

The language we learned when we were in school
    can be very useful, as a rule
To be a sports fan, you must add much more
    or else you may end up not knowing the score

When a baseball batter has a "Sacrifice" fly
    No, it doesn't mean someone is going to die.
A pitcher may throw a "Split-Fingered" fast ball
    It really doesn't mean what it sounds like, at all.

In basketball a "Double Dribble" sounds as if
    The player could use a handkerchief
They also call "Goal Tending" in this game
    In hockey or soccer it doesn't mean the same.

Why in hockey is "Icing the Puck" not good?
    It's always on the ice, they don't play on wood.
"High Sticking" is also a move to abhor
    I'd think "Low Sticking" would hurt much more.

In football, "Clipping" is a call they all fear
    You can kill from the front, but not from the rear
"Pass Interference" the refs will not condone.
    Is the defense supposed to leave them alone?

In golf, "Birdie and Eagle" are often heard words
    Is that why duffers cry: "My game's for the birds"?
If you're not up to "Par", you may be sick
    In golf, it means you goofed with the stick

In boxing a "Technical" knockout is feared
    By "Technical" do they mean it's been engineered?
Don't let "Bantamweight" or "Featherweight" fool you a bit
    They may be small, but they know how to hit.

Don't despair, if these terms leave you lame.
    Just turn off the sound, and enjoy the game.

THE SPORT OF STRINGS

Of all the sports to watch on TV
    Tennis is the most enjoyable for me
In addition to the great matches you see
    each player has a distinct personality

First everyone's favorite, Jimmy Connors
    as a competitor, he gets the honors
When young, he was called "the brat"
    with maturity, he's almost gotten over that

Speaking of brats, there's John McEnroe
    Childish behavior he doesn't outgrow
Despite it all, I've got to say
    it's a lot of fun watching John play

Andre Agassi strikes mighty blows
    How does he do it, wearing those clothes?
His long hair dazzles the younger crowd
    I didn't think ear rings were allowed!

Yvan Lendl, a stoic he is called
    His serve leaves the opponents appalled
His money winnings are tops, by heck
    Not bad for a transplanted Czech.

Boris Becker, the German ace
    has spent many seasons in first place
His athletic prowess is very well known
    his ball speed approaches the supersonic zone

There's just room to mention the rest of the gang
    like Sampras, Edberg, Courier and Chang

For great women tennis stars credit is also due
    I'd like to review just a few:
Steffi Graff's first name should have been Hans
    Her overhead smash is just like a man's
Evert is one we're all going to miss
    For years there was a winner named Chris

Continued

Martina Navratalova is at the top of her game
    Too bad nothing rhymes with her last name
Gabriela Sabatini's skill may often be seen
    She's both a tennis and a beauty queen
Monica Seles plays with much poise
    Does she have to make all that noise?
Jennifer Capriati is the latest young rage
    Imagine her game when she comes of age!

I've reluctantly accepted that tennis is not my sport
    My age is too long, and my breath is too short

SATURDAY MORNING BLUES

With a loud groan, and a gaping yawn
    I forced myself out of bed at dawn
Gulp down breakfast, mustn't be late
    for our early Saturday morning golf date
Speed to the course, pay the greens fee
    All of this rush to be first on the tee
We swing and we sway at break of day
    that's the way we grown-ups play
If you shift your body, like you hadn't ought-er
    splash, your ball ends up in the water
Move your head, or lock your knees
    Wham, your drive is in the trees
Putting looks simple, but it isn't at all
    The hole always seems to miss my ball
On rare occasions, you shoot a good score
    That's what makes you come back for more
Sometimes a question races through my head
    Would I be better off if I "stood in bed"?

WHAT AM I BID?

As I read those very detailed reports
    of player negotiations in professional sports
I'm reminded of stockyard auctions of cattle
    where bidding for beef is quite a battle
The only difference that I can scent
    is the steers don't have agents who take ten percent.

TOO MANY SPORTS

Professional sports are on a collision course
    especially in April and May
Hockey and basketball are still playing off
    and baseball takes place every day

In addition to those, we see golf pros
    competing on greens every week
Tournaments of tennis, from Paris to Venice
    are there, if diversion you seek

Furthermore, you can now keep score
    in stadium football for also-rans
Nobody knows, how they can support these shows
    There are almost more athletes than fans!

GOLFER'S LAMENT

"If you want to relax, play golf", they said.
    Here is what I discovered instead:
Water holes try your souls
    A bad slice ain't very nice
Out-of-bounds ruins your rounds
    Heavy rough is too darned tough
Sand traps, your temper snaps
    Penalties drive you to your knees
A friendly bet, I haven't won yet

While "Senior" is a respectful term
    and the senior golf tour is nifty
How can they call themselves "senior"
    when they've only reached the age of fifty?

Golf is called a gentleman's sport
    Not everyone can easily be taught
The reason my golf game is so shoddy
    My brains ain't connected to my body!

Golf is a game you should approach
    with serious dedication, plus a good coach
If neither of these improves your play
    join the crowd, and enjoy it anyway.

If you must play golf, heed this plea
    Don't watch tournaments on TV
Now matter how skillful you may think you've become
    watching the pros makes you feel like a bum.

It's bad enough to land in the rough
    after almost every drive
It hurts much more, and ruins your score
    when your putts just don't arrive

If, in Florida, you're a baseball buff
    spring training doesn't last long enough
Just when you get to know their names
    they go up north to play real games

You may get to feel out of sorts
    and can tire yourself out in sports
But you've never felt real fatigue
    until you try coaching Little League.

Sports used to be my obsession
 For all home teams I was a rooter
I no longer show any favoritism
 Like our family dog, I'm neuter.

British sports are an enigma to me
 Like cricket and the battle called rugby
Cricket is gentlemanly in the A.M. or P.M.
 Rugby is a form of disorganized mayhem.

NHL, PBA, NBA, and PGA
 They're all groups of pro athletes who play
games just like we do on a weekend day
 But they sure play for lots more pay.

Baseball players must be aggressive
 There are hitters, stealers, and bunters
Their defensive training now includes
 protection from autograph hunters

Fishing is a most relaxing sport
 Whether you catch many, or come home with naught
In either event, I'm pleased to report
 I found the peace and quiet I sought.

Whenever I watch a game on TV
 and somebody makes a great score
Instead of showing the players involved
 They switch to the crowd, what for?

If pro basketball is your passion
 and you tire of your wife's plaintive song
Just watch the very end of the contest
 The real game's only five minutes long.

"No one likes a loser"
    I heard Our football coach yell
After losing fifteen games
    he lost his job as well.

―――――――

Football and baseball are organized sports.
    To play them you must be mental.
Ice hockey and soccer are something else
    The goals always look accidental.

―――――――

Guns may be very important
    for police and military use
But why so many firearms
    just to shoot a poor duck or a goose?

―――――――

Go visit a bowling alley
    There are interesting sights to see
After the ball is on its way
    They guide it with head, hips, and knee.

―――――――

Little League baseball is hard to believe
    To fathom it I have been trying
If they win, their enthusiasm is hard to control
    When they lose, you can't stop their crying!

―――――――

One thing that always puzzles me
    as I stare at my TV screen
"He pitched a split-fingered fast ball"
    Is that what they really mean?

―――――――

We went to a Super Bowl party
    All of our close friends came
We ate, and drank, and talked for hours
    and forgot to watch the game

Here come all the decorated floats
 and bands too numerous to name
There's so much football, for so many weeks
 The parade is often better than the game

Of all the sports there are to see
 boxing is not my "cup of tea"
Wrestling is ranked even further behind it
 It's obviously fixed, but their fans don't mind it.

I'd like to forget, all the money I've bet
 on a baseball play-off game
Whatever the odds, I pick all the clods
 I'm in the "Losers" Hall of Fame!

I used to read the sports pages
 to see who won and how
Lately all I seem to read about
 are the millions they're making now.

Skiing may be O.K. for some
 who enjoy being frozen and numb
My daughter should heed what I taught 'er
 It's much warmer skiing on water!

Football is usually played outdoors
 with wind, sleet, and snow in the open
Those cheerleaders aren't dressed very warm
 They won't catch pneumonia, I'm hopin'

I jogged every morning, sunshine or rain.
 Like all the others, I would puff, wheeze, and strain.
Now I walk every day at a leisurely pace
 I traded the pain for the smile on my face.

We follow our minor league baseball team
 and enjoy it, whatever the score
Young players on the way up, oldsters going down
 Like escalators in a department store

Whatever sport I choose to watch
 as I look at the TV pictures
Up front, there's always a long-haired man
 with a big sign, citing the scriptures
Regardless of how you personally feel
 about religion or that persistent gent
it hardly seems the appropriate time
 for us to relent or repent.

Pumps were used for tires and balloons
 now they're involved in what we wear
Inflatable shoes for running, pump-up bras for sunning
 These new fashions are full of hot air!

I would not want you to think I am bitter
 but who dreamed up the "designated hitter"?
American League pitcher's hitting is very irrational
 when they're traded to the League that's National.

Athlete's salaries have gotten out of hand
 The weakest performers make two hundred grand
It's an oxymoron that tries my patience
 How dare they call themselves "free" agents?

ON THE
ROAD AGAIN

ON THE ROAD AGAIN

During my business career, I made it very clear
    since I had travelled the country wide
When my work was done, no more would I run
    All my luggage I planned to hide

Forget the trains, the crowded planes
    the airports, hotels, and such
"I'm home, dear wife, for the rest of our life.
    No more airline food will I touch"

"Welcome home, dear spouse", said the lady of the house
    "Relax, let your nerves unravel"
I didn't realize, and she took me by surprise
    saying: "It's finally my turn to travel"

After years of home-making, cooking, and baking
    while I flew the coop all week
I should have known, now the children have flown
    escape from her prison she'd seek.

Fishing and golf were on my mind
    Instead travel brochures I'd find
Little did I know when I decided to retire
    My wife longed to be a "frequent flyer"

Our home was designed with comfort in mind
    Why would anyone leave this behind?
In order to be fair we took a vote
    She won by one, I sadly must note.

Off we went, as tourists will
    to California, Europe, and even Brazil
Before each trip was hardly done
    She had already planned the very next one

A sad thing I found, as we toured around
    and it's quite a bitter pill
Wherever we went, my own money I spent
    The company no longer picked up the bill!

Here's my advice, stop and think twice
    before you retire, heed this poem
Don't be a jerk, continue to work
    At least you'll spend weekends at home.

THE JOY OF FLYING?

I can't understand why so many folks maintain
    they're afraid to fly, and take the bus or a train
As for me, flying is fast and the planes are great
    It's the little annoyances that I've come to hate.

You get there quickly, I can't deny
    That's really the only reason to fly
But while you're flyin', it's very tryin'
    If the ads claim you'll relax, they're lyin'

The trip to the airport, I must confess
    in heavy traffic, can be a big mess
But finally it's time to board the plane
    That's when the trouble starts, let me explain:

I've checked my bags, then let out a moan
    The rest come aboard carrying everything they own
They strain, and push, and the overheads stuff
    Why don't they realize "Enough is enough!"?

To start off the trip on a happy note
    the stewardess explains how seat cushions float
"Are you all comfortable"?, they cheerily ask
    then they describe your oxygen mask!

When we start to taxi, there's no going back
    My neighbor needs something from the overhead rack
The seat belt sign's on, as everyone knows
    But he gets up anyway, and crushes my toes

The businessman sits with his attache case
    with a look of boredom on his face
As luck would have it, the seat he chose
    is next to a brat with a runny nose

As the children their toys noisily unfold
    I have a suggestion, if I may be so bold
Regardless of whether it's hot or it's cold
    the airline should seat kids in the baggage hold.

Continued

Whenever I have an urge to take a snooze
    I'm stuck beside a gent who is full of booze
It's particularly annoying to me, because
    I get the story of his life, without a pause

Furthermore, whenever I need to go to the john
    the captain quickly puts the seat belt sign on
When I finally went, I'm sorry to say
    some violent turbulence ruined my day

The "White-knuckle" fliers lose their poise
    each time there's a change in the engine noise
I guess fear of flying isn't so funny
    Although you get airsick, they still keep your money

When I finally doze, it doesn't last long
    The energetic stewardesses sing their song
Pushing their cart smack into my knee
    cheerfully asking: "Coffee, milk, or tea"?

They used to serve meals, now they give you a "snack"
    If I wasn't so hungry, I'd send it right back
In the process of removing the tight plastic wrap
    I spilled half the contents into my lap

We finally descended, and landed with a roar
    Everyone jostled to be first out the door
The baggage area was a mile from our gate
    Despite that, we still had more time to wait

The story doesn't end there, I'm sorry to say
    One major annoyance to ruin my day
The baggage handler advised, with some pity
    my bag had gone on to some other city!

DEALS ON WHEELS

After your car is well broken in
    and all the repairs are made
You wake up one day, and have to say
    It's too old, for a new one I'll trade

No need to go far to shop for a car
    the phone book lists four dozen dealers
It'll take till next fall to see them all
    I'll pick some and put out feelers.

They all have "deals" for their automobiles
    It sounds too good to be true
Discounts, rebates, and low cost loans
    "I've got a real bargain for you".

When I bought my last car, prices were high
    or so I thought years before.
The prices today, will make your head sway
    Twice as expensive, and more

Then I inquired "Is it white wall tired?"
    "FM radio and air-conditioning?"
I asked him twice: "Is it in the price?"
    The salesman didn't seem to be listening.

"Let's talk about trading my old car in.
    It's clean and has been handled with care"
They offered me half of it's value
    That's why they preach: "Buyer beware"

"Let's talk turkey" I finally said
    "How much will I really spend?"
"For this expensive new car you offer
    and when will the payments end?"

For some strange reason they always go
    in the back room to work out the price
Are they really consulting the manager
    or just keeping me "on ice"?

Despite my fears, I went into arrears
    Drove the new car home with shame
For the money it cost, our vacation was lost
    They call it playing the "American Game".

MISGUIDED TOURS

Vacations used to be simple, we'd pack the car
    gather the kids, drive no matter how far
Off to the mountains, or perhaps to the beach
    We settled down, relaxed, and stayed within reach

Relaxing vacations are a thing of the past
    We now take tours, expensive and fast
On plane, train, and bus we travel afar
    Oh, to be back in our family car

You are guided through each city, from end to end
    and nowhere do they give you leisure time to spend
You pack and unpack, you mutter and fuss
    Bolt down your breakfast, then back on the bus

The tour director rattles off what we will next see
    Where we will eat and sleep in what country
After a while, (and I think I've gone lame)
    The museums and churches all look the same

At one of our stops, I tried my best
    to find a quiet corner, cold beer, and some rest
The tour director found me, and said to the crowd:
    "I thought I explained this isn't allowed"

I hasten to add, despite my glum mood
    The accommodations were fine, and so was the food
But vacations are supposed to be restful and relaxing
    I found guided tours very tiring and taxing

Although we had signed up for a tour that was guided
    when I got home, I definitely decided
to become a "conscientious objector"
    the next time I meet a tour director.

WHY ME?

When school vacation used to arrive
    we'd run out with baseball in hand
Today that's no longer the thing to do
    We must all rush to Disneyland

No longer do kids want to frolic and roam
    in the fields around our house
Priorities have changed, it's been all arranged
    by a character named Mickey Mouse.

Cancel all your business engagements
    Make plane and hotel arrangements
If that's not enough to add to your woes
    for this trip everyone must have new clothes

Orlando used to be, a non-entity
    where oranges and cattle were grown
There's none of that left, the fields are bereft
    They now raise hotels of stone

Finally we all trouped to Disney's land
    Children clutching us by the hand
Enjoyed a fancy marching band
    Filled the gang up at the popcorn stand

The first attraction we wanted to see
    didn't look too crowded to me
But inside they waited in a complex maze
    People looked like they'd been there for days

Oh well, we came to have some fun
    Our visit has just barely begun
If waiting in line is what we must do
    I'll accept the inevitable, wouldn't you?

I have to tell you now we're outside
    We waited an hour for a ten minute ride
The sun is so hot, we're all getting fried
    I wish I could find somewhere to hide

Continued

The children were thrilled, I must repeat
    as long as they always had something to eat
We finally found a show with a seat
    What a treat to get off my feet

I hasten to add, if I sound like a bore
    We got just what we bargained for
I really didn't realize what was in store
    After a long day, the kids still wanted "more"

After many restaurants, and gift shops too
    we finally ran out of things to do
The children wanted to continue to roam
    All I could think of was "Home Sweet Home"

A visit to Disneyland will surely cost you
    about as much as a trip to France or Peru
That's a lot of money to spend on a lark
    at a big, noisy, overgrown amusement park

TRAVEL TIPS

During my career, travelling country-wide
    There wasn't an airline on which I did not ride
As I moved around, pursuing my profession
    certain big cities left quite an impression

Boston's a seaport, and a center of learning
    and can satisfy your seafood yearning
A high tech center, without a doubt
    Once there, traffic jams won't let you out

There's no place like New York, all agree
    You have to go to Central Park to see a tree
For great theater, it's the very top
    But don't walk the streets without a cop

Chicago, a big town on Michigan Lake
    You'll freeze if warm clothes you don't take
The people and the steaks are very rare
    Enjoy them if you ever get out of O'Hare

Continued

In Atlanta, you can have a ball
    despite all the Georgians who say "you-all"
It's very cosmopolitan for a southern city
    If you don't eat grits, they show no pity

Seattle is almost too beautiful to describe
    Everything from Mount Rainier to an Indian tribe
The views are magnificent every day
    Why does it have to be so far away?

Houston is a very macho place
    Everyone follows the NFL race
It's heat and humidity can make you broil
    Their major exports are politicians and oil.

Our nation's capitol is something you must see
    It has alternating current, but is called "D.C."
A visit to Washington is a worthwhile journey
    particularly if you're a politician or attorney.

Los Angeles is like some movie plots
    The freeways are all big parking lots
It's always exciting, both day and night
    That is, if the smog doesn't ruin your sight

San Francisco is a favorite stop of mine
    I rush to the Wharf, on seafood to dine
It's best described in Tony Bennett's song
    Once you visit Frisco, you'll be back before long

To live in Buffalo you must be strong
    Their winter lasts all the year long
In that climate, I don't belong
    I hope Buffalonians don't take this wrong

Miami, a truly international location
    Where many from the northeast take their vacation
The beaches are fine, if a suntan you seek
    It's also helpful, if Spanish you speak

Minneapolis people are a pleasure to know
    They fish and they boat, despite all that snow
If you plan to visit, remember one thing
    Hold off your trip until summer or spring

Continued

New Orleans is in the very deep south
    Where Mississippi seafood will please your mouth
The heat and humidity is "out of sight!"
    That's why Bourbon Street is crowded only at night

I'd like to include others in this anthology
    If your city was omitted, accept my apology.

DEJA VU

In my working years, I spun my gears
    travelling coast to coast like a flash
I could hardly wait for my retirement date
    My luggage would go in the trash

That day is now here, I sighed loud and clear
    as I surveyed my workshop and yard
No more travel, my nerves could unravel
    then I tore up my airline travel card

My devoted spouse, welcomed me to our house
    with a very enthusiastic tone
"Our children have fled", she happily said
    "And now I'm no longer alone"

In no small measure, I enjoyed my leisure
    Joining all the golfing fans
Then to my surprise, she hit me between the eyes
    Saying "Let's discuss our travel plans"

"I've been stuck in this place", she threw in my face
    "While you have been gadding about"
"While you kept going, the lawn I've been mowing"
    "It's my turn to gad", she did shout.

Needless to say, my wife got her way
    On my street, our garden looks poorest
Once again I live out of a suitcase
    I have become a tourist!

A two week vacation actually takes a month
    The two mid-weeks offer pleasure and thrills
but it takes a week to prepare for your trip
    and a fourth week to pay all the bills!

More and more, the young ignore
    the "Rules 0f the Road" in their driving
That's probably the main reason for
    auto body shops all thriving

Airlines print detailed timetables
    with departure times planned to the minute
Oh, the plane may depart the gate right on time
    but on the runway for an hour you sit in it!

If human beings were meant to fly
    they'd have wings to soar up to the sky
Alas, airplanes must take us from place to place
    But birds fly with so much more grace.

I decided to bring my car in for repair
    Smiling "Mr. Goodwrench" greeted me there
A simple tune-up will fix it, I innocently thought
    The bill was worth half of the car I had bought

License plates were designed to provide
    identification for your car as you ride
Vanity plated seem stupid to be buying
    especially if being incognito you are trying

A good rule to remember, I am told
    "The left one is hot, the right is cold"
Hotel showers, especially in the morning
    turn freezing cold, without any warning.

Super highways cross the land
    They're crowded day and night
Most drivers think those extra lanes
    were designed to "pass on the right"

The auto ads now proudly state
    a computer runs every new car
If they "glitch" like the computer at home
    the new cars will not go very far.

If you're like me, when your car stalls
    you rush out and lift up the hood
You stare, and poke, and try to look smart
    but it never does any good.

Travel is quite educational
    Especially if your route is extensive
But travel like college can take its toll
    They're both extremely expensive

Planes are crowded, highways jammed
    Cities are paralyzed with traffic
I think we'll do our travelling
    at home with National Geographic

When I bought a car I used to know
    it would simply take me where I had to go
Be prepared when today's new car you enter
    It is now a computerized entertainment center

Youngsters in sports cars always have
    their radio speakers turned up all the way
While it may make me very uncomfortable
    they will be deaf someday!

On many roads, the country wide
    "Deer Crossing" signs I see.
I sometimes wonder who they're for
    The crossing deer or me?

"Right Turn on Red" is now the law
    Through most of the U.S.A.
At red lights I find, I'm stuck behind
    drivers who don't go that way

I sit in stalled traffic at the bridge
    "A Pox" on boats is my fervent wish
Why should one hundred people wait
    so one guy with a boat can catch fish?

Some folks have a radar detector
    they mount in their cars secretly
If they plan to exceed the speed limit
    I detect no protection for me.

I always drive at fifty-five
    This directive is something I heed
But lately I have the suspicion
    It's become the "minimum" speed.

It's hard to figure out what to do
    when I read those signs around town.
Since my car only runs horizontally
    Do I slow "up", or do I slow "down"?

There's one thing about my car, I find
    with any mechanic that I know
If one little part has acted up
    seven others will then let go!

THE SOCIAL HOUR

"BRIDGE" OF SIGHS

A social evening used to be
    small talk and a raid on the fridge'
But now as soon as the sun goes down
    my friends say "Let's play bridge"

Now I can enjoy a friendly game
    of poker, or rummy called gin
But those who say, bridge is fun to play
    have committed a mortal sin

In college I, was urged to try
    this game, I won't deny
but in that day, I learned to play
    the Culbertson rules of Ely

Today they don't use simple rules
    As they sit around the table
A complicated point system now prevails
    To explain it, I'm not able

Here's a new rub, you bid one club
    Do you mean one club? No way!
It's a new rule, your opponents to fool
    And seems the wrong thing to say

I'm no fool, here's another rule
    I can't neglect to mention
If your hand's a bust, you can I trust
    make up a new "convention"

Each day in our local paper
    the bridge column is on page nine
Who understands, with such terrible hands
    How they make slam every time

Friendly discussions are fun for me
    at home, at work, or when walking
But when bridge hands are dealt out
    They glare if they catch you talking

Continued

I still play bridge my very own way
　　They can leave it, or they can take it
I bid six hearts, my partner throws darts
　　Who cares, I always make it

Here's my approach to playing bridge
　　when the inevitable seems to face me
I immediately yell, "I don't feel well"
　　And they find someone to replace me.

SOCIAL MISCONDUCT

Before we leave for a party
　　my wife lays down the law
On how to act, and use more tact
　　But, wait, there's a whole lot more

"Religion and politics are no-nos"
　　"Don't bore them with your last operation"
"No off-color jokes, will you tell these folks,
　　or we'll have a trial separation"

"Don't argue all night about football"
　　"or complain about our marriage"
I've never had so many instructions
　　since I left my baby carriage!

To avoid a row, I kept my vow
　　I was quiet as a mime's double
and stuck to eating, instead of speaking
　　Let other husbands get into trouble

DARNED IF YOU DO

Whenever Joe wants to play poker
    his wife shouts "You can't leave this house"
He obeys her command without question
    He's not a man, he's a "mouse".

His friend pays his spouse no attention
    goes out alone every night to carouse
His wife is never home either
    This "man" owns an empty house.

The moral of this sad story
    is to always go out with your spouse.
and that will settle the issue.
    You'll be both a "man" and a "mouse".

I shout "Hurry up" to my wife
    who is upstairs donning her gown
It sounds absurd, I should change a word
    and ask her to please hurry "down"

Neighborhood friends will flock around
    when it's privacy you desire
More guests you'll see, particularly
    when you light the charcoal fire

"Company tonight?", I asked my spouse
    "How did you know?", I heard her grouse
I think I'll be quiet as a mouse
    It's the only time she cleans the house

I happened to come home early one day
    Heard my wife and a bridge game in play
From the tone of the conversation, I reckoned
    Gossip comes first, bridge comes second

I hear them preach, don't dare reach
    for a drink, though the day may drag so
But as soon as the clock strikes 5 P.M.
    On your mark, get set, let's go!

I'm not impressed, with an unwelcome guest
    who drops in on us without warning
I'm even less excited, with someone we invited
    who drinks and talks until morning.

If you take a hard drink, but have nothing to eat
    why those snide looks, if you please?
But a snort is respectable, even delectable
    if you have it with crackers and cheese

At a party, though she's two rooms away
    my wife can listen, and contradict what I say
But when we're alone, she turns a deaf ear
    to everything I really want her to hear.

A "Vanity" is where a wife stores her supplies
    to satisfy her "vanity", painting lips, face, and eyes
Husbands are a different branch of humanity
    waiting for her to finish gives rise to profanity

Some friends are loyal, some are not
    Many push their friendship too far
Several I don't consider my friends at all
    They're "fiends" if you drop the "r"

The cocktail "hour" is wrongly named
    if grammar is your line
Why do we call it the cocktail hour
    when it lasts from six to nine?

People make such a ritual of mixing martinis
  Preparing them takes longer and longer
Do they really taste better than other drinks?
  No, the truth is martinis are stronger!

Ordering a "martini" is quite respectable
  "Straight gin" sounds very uncouth
To be considered a classy drinker, not an alcoholic
  involves just a dash of vermouth.

HOME OWNERS LAMENT

CONDO-"MINIMUMS"

Up north a house is where you lived
    All seasons through the year
And everything about that place
    Was yours to domineer

Now you're retired, and gave that up
    and moved to Condo land
Down south where winter never comes
    to frolic in sun and sand

No more to worry when you will
    cut grass or plow the walk
or paint the house or fix the roof
    just eat and drink and talk.

"But, what is this?" you say one day
    Our home we don't truly own
We share it all with folks galore
    Who are always on the phone

The committee says we can't do this
    or that which we may decide
Majority rules our every move
    "Don't park that boat outside"

We used to fix our home at times
    When finances allowed
But now we must adhere to rules
    of the rest of the Condo crowd

It seems that we started out this life
    with rules set by fathers and mothers
And now we finally have retired
    to rules still set by others

Oh Condo life, it sounds so great
    In that full-color flyer
But don't believe everything you read
    As you prepare to retire

Beware as you mail your money in
    and pause as you paste on a stamp
Do you really want the Condo life?
    In a retiree's "army camp."

DO WHAT YOURSELF ?

"Do-it-yourself" I used to say
    when the cost of repairmen grew dear
Why should I, those high prices pay?
    I've got time, and the hardware store's near

In a mad buying spree, I shopped merrily
    for tools, and nails, and such
Each gadget I saw, I bought at the store
    Why not?, I'll be saving so much.

Next day cried my wife in obvious strife
    "Help, the roof's sprung a leak"
The new ladder I scaled, but my hard labor failed
    It better not rain for a week.

I next attempted to fix the plumbing
    and electric wires tried to splice
I can tell you now, I didn't know how
    and everything's broken down twice.

I'll pass on some advice to you
    when you read those home repair books
in spite of the step-by-step pictures
    "It ain't as easy as it looks!"

If I could reclaim the money I spent
    On all that "fix-it yourself" gear
For goodness sake, a profit I'd make
    paying repairmen all through the year.

HOME BUYERS LAMENT

Why oh why did I ever buy
    This house, it's making me poor
I should have picked a place to live
    with a handyman next door

I must confess, it's true I guess
    My trouble is self-inflicted
This house is my responsibility
    'Cause I'm the one who picked it

We liked the view, and the neighbors too
    The price was quite affordable
We ignored the floors, didn't test the doors
    but the deed was deemed recordable

I should have sensed some trouble
    when we met the owners to buy
They wished us well, then ran like hell
    before the ink was dry

Like babes in the woods, we moved our goods
    So what if the floors were squeaking
But what is this? Something is amiss
    It rained and the roof is leaking!

I phoned the local roofer
    to please come out that day
He sympathized, then I closed my eyes
    For a new roof I'll have to pay

All muddy we, decided to flee
    to the shower to make us neater
I let out a shout, and jumped right out
    What's wrong with the hot water heater?

Oh, that's not all, I "climbed the wall"
    after calling the real estate whiz
"You may be pained", he quickly explained
    "But you bought the house 'as-is' "

THE REAL-TY TRUTH

To sell your house, the experts say
    A realtor you have to hire
Don't take a chance, you may lose your pants
    if "sell-it-yourself" you desire

We said O.K., we'll try your way
    A realtor was asked to begin
To use their advertised expertise
    and parade all the buyers in.

From stem to stern we cleaned our house
    and sat back to await the flow
of prospects anxious to move right in
    with their checkbooks ready to go.

The hours, and days, and weeks went by
    No activity could we see.
If realtors are really the way to go
    They didn't prove it to me.

"The market's slow, your price is high"
    They hemmed, and hawed, and whined.
Where were all these problems
    when they urged our contract be signed?

Another sales approach they took
    "You're in the Multiple Listing Book"
After ninety days with no-one to look
    Like amateur night, we gave them the "hook"

Now I've nothing against realtors
    But their promises give me a pain
This experience forced a decision
    In this "saleable" house we'll remain.

Gardening used to be lots of fun
    up north where the seasons were clear
Down south it's summer all the time
    and weeds grow throughout the year

We wash and clean each window
    until not a spot remains
Then we cover them up with drapes and blinds
    Why did we go to such pains?

You may run out of cash or run out of gas
    or even deplete pantry stores
What we never seem to run out of
    are those miserable household chores

I used to have a very "green thumb"
    but that I can no longer say
Like me, my plants are growing old
    and my lawn is turning gray.

You may enjoy tiling a floor
    But as for me, nevermore!

A swimming pool may be great to own
    Most people have never seen it
They may be the lucky ones
    They don't have to daily clean it.

It's hard to like, your neighbor's tyke
    when he ruins your flower garden
When he grows up he'll answer to
    his jailers and the warden

Whenever I'm forced to paint a room
    There's a job from which I must shirk
I don't mind covering the ceiling and walls
    but I can't stand doing woodwork!

————————

Authors crow, of the splendors of snow
    as it covers each hill, house, and tree
I might agree, this beauty to see
    if those writers would shovel the snow for me

————————

Spring up north is very welcome
    when plants and flowers start to grow
But I can't keep myself from thinking
    of the lawn soon ready to mow

————————

There's something about owning a home
    that turns a smile into a frown
Just when you have everything working right
    something else is sure to break down

————————

We always liked to play our part
    and filled our home with modern art
Our art appreciation has a new call
    Grandchildren's photos cover each wall

————————

Up north they call it a porch
    In Florida we have lanais
One thing they have in common
    A screen to keep out the flies

————————

I fuss and fertilize and water my garden
    Try every trick that I know
And still I can't get good results
    Some flowers just don't want to grow

There's a question I often ask
    Whenever I tackle a household task
If I drop my tools and hit the hay
    Will the problem go away?

————————

You can develop a very sore thorax
    from scrubbing the floor with Borax

————————

Solar energy may be our last resort
    to use when the Earth turns cool
Too bad we only use it today
    to heat the swimming pool

————————

Shrubs all start to grow in June
    I'm afraid it's now the time to prune
Prune is a name that really suits
    My least favorite of all dried fruits

————————

We curse, and sweat, and bemoan our fate
    as we mow the lawn, early and late
Then we rush to the garden store
    for fertilizer, so it'll grow even more

————————

Of cleaning products, I've tried quite a few
    but none seem to get rid of mildew
If people wouldn't think I'm a dullard
    I'd paint everything mildew-colored!

————————

On a sunny day our newspaper is found
    at the door, right at our feet
Whenever the rain comes pouring down
    it's tossed in the middle of the street

————————

If you complain every time you mow
    stop watering and fertilizing, the grass won't grow
But then the weeds will take over your yard
    and then you'll complain twice as hard

White carpets, white tile floor
    show every speck of dirt, door to door
Still we must maintain our home in fashion
    Daily with vacuum, broom, and mop we're dashin'

I miss the small local hardware shops
    You bought what you needed, no more
The new super "do-it-yourself" depots
    are a temptation to buy out the store

Everyone complained, but I wasn't listening
    when I decided to turn off the air conditioning
To survive this heat takes a really firm will
    Especially after paying my electric bill!

Sooner or later, you must face the truth
    carpets don't last forever, just like your youth
The ads all said it would never stain
    That may be true, if completely off it you remain

The spring flowers in our garden
    are resplendent in every color
Just waiting for bees to visit
    Their sex life couldn't be duller.

CAN'T STOP SHOPPING

THE NEW SHOPPING NETWORK

They used to steer the ship of state
    and gave businesses a good start
but now retired, they find themselves
    pushing a shopping cart

Up and down the market's aisles
    these retirees explore
They're having trouble finding
    what's carried in each store

Some men can't seem to get the hang
    of shopping, let's be kind
You see them following Grandma
    Pushing their carts behind

But others venture out alone
    With lists in both their hands
They know exactly what they need
    But why so many brands?

This one's on sale, and that one's not
    A calculator's needed
If you can find the coupons
    at savings you've succeeded

Ho, what is this, a chocolate bar?
    your list did not include
What the heck, I'll take a chance
    and sneak it home with the food

At last the list is all complete
    To the checkout line I go
Which line to choose?, no time to lose
    Most are far too slow

The line I picked looked very short
    I beat the game, by heck
Too late to find, I got behind
    Three women who each wrote a check

I must admit, I worked or played
    while my spouse performed these chores
I never dreamed what was involved
    in refilling our kitchen stores.

"PRESENTS" OF MIND

Families are great, don't get me wrong
    but we seem to buy presents all year long
A greeting card always used to be sufficient
    Today, if that's all you send, you're considered deficient

Birthdays, anniversaries, graduations and more
    Keeps our charge accounts active at each local store
Of spouses, children, grandchildren, in-laws I speak
    There's an occasion to celebrate almost every week

Good friends must be included in the shopping list
    plus aunts, uncles, and cousins who shouldn't be missed
Mothers and fathers days have become a craze
    No wonder they call them "Hallmark Holidays"

Engagements and weddings add fuel to the fire
    and presents for those who decide to retire
Then through the gift shops we have to roam
    for friends who have finally bought a new home

That's only the beginning of shopping I fear
    In the wink of an eye, Christmas is here!
That old adage is hard to believe
    Is it really better to give than receive?

DON'T FALL FOR A MALL

One of the ventures I avoid most of all
    is attempting to shop at the new giant mall.
No matter the season, shoppers fill the place
    That is, after they've fought for a parking place
If clothing stores you're after, there are dozens to choose
    and six places sell nothing but sneakers and shoes
Books, food, or jewelry, you will find them all there
    Gift shops and toy stores are everywhere
As for me, I still shop at each neighborhood store
    where the owners know me, I've been there before
No music or crowds, no clerks that are bored
    Just good service and clothing that I can afford.
The problem, my friend, I'm beginning to hear
    malls are causing local shops to disappear
If this keeps up, and they all fall
    the only shopping will be at the mall.
I guess I could always revert to past years
    and order most things from the catalogue of Sears!

We now shop at a "Warehouse"
    for bargains we like to roam
You save the most if you buy a gross
    We now have a "warehouse" at home.

Do not fall for a telephone call
    when they offer you something free.
In order to get it, they must check your credit
    Then they sell you a new policy

Designer jeans are quite the thing
    They're too tight and all in blue tones
Our young people like to look alike
    I call them "designer" clones.

Clothing ads say it's the latest rage
   My wife rushes out to get it
To me, a "rage" is what I felt
   When she used up my line of credit.

Mail order products seem very low priced
   and many buyers are therefore enticed
I'll let you in on a secret, honey
   "Postage and Handling" is where they make their money

It seems that every store gives a discount
   Their entire stock is always on sale
That's why I can't get excited
   when I open up all that junk mail.

Every time I use a credit card
   my phone number I must write
Maybe that's how those telephone salesmen
   know where to reach me each night.

How do you buy at a bargain
   with prices that never seem low?
You could go wrong, if you take too long
   The big sale was two weeks ago

Investment opportunities are many
   A rich speculator I'd like to be
But in buying hog belly futures
   I can't see a future for me

If you'd like to dress in high fashion
   I'll expose one of their fables
Women don't choose the best looking attire
   No, most of them shop for "labels"

The reason people flock to garage sales
    (and this is quite easy to prove)
is to buy up lots of old junk
    for their garage sale when they move

Refund coupons are all the rage
    You find them on almost every page
If you read the fine print, under a lamp
    it's not much more than the new postage stamp

Mail order is a curious business
    no matter what product you get
It's "Allow 8 weeks for delivery"
    I bet they haven't produced it yet!

Shopping malls seem to be
    places where many couples flee
Wives shop, husbands sit or pace
    Take my advice, avoid the place.

THE MONEY GAME

A RUN ON YOUR MONEY

On paper you add up your income
    and total expenses to pay
It looks like there's plenty left over
    but it never works out that way.

You cover the rent and buy the food
    then pay the local utility
Accounting for everything else
    is an exercise in futility.

We're both working, so do not fret
    Our income's multiplied by two
That doesn't seem to be much help
    When all the insurance is due.

If some day you find spare cash
    I warn you, don't get lax
when next you trot to your mailbox
    Oops, here comes the Income Tax!

When your wife doesn't ask for money
    don't get too serene
She's doing just as much spending
    Using the Automatic Teller Machine.

If you're careful when you go shopping
    Finding bargains isn't so hard
But that doesn't help when the time comes
    to pay off your credit card.

We tried very strict budgeting
    Wrote every expense in a book
Our bank account still kept shrinking
    Whenever we dared to look.

No matter what your income
    I've become resigned to say
If a dollar comes in, two quickly go out
    I guess that's the American way.

BANKER'S HOLIDAY

Let's be frank, to choose a bank
    is a challenge most mysterious
They all claim they're the very best
    But my questions remain serious

C.D.'s, I.R.A.'s, loans and trusts
    Their list of services mount.
Hold your fire, all I desire
    is a savings and checking account

It must be nice to work in a bank
    While we all like a paid holiday
The bankers use, the slightest excuse
    to keep their doors shut all day.

Since most people labor from nine to five
    there's one thing I can't see.
If banks really want to serve us best
    Why only work from ten to three?

I finally decided they're all the same
    and selected a bank, to my shame
not for their rates, or interest dates
    but the one who remembered my name.

IT AIN'T EASY

Money can be made in different ways
    You can earn it by laboring all of your days
Counterfeiters print it, but that doesn't pay
    They'll jail you and throw the key away
Invest in the stock market, if you choose
    In this economy, your shirt you may lose
Real estate profits once rang the bell
    Now you may buy, but nothing will sell
It's no wonder (and pardon my rambling)
    that so many people have taken up gambling
You may choose horse races, your money to blow
    The odds on the winners are pitifully low
Most states now have lotteries, with a fortune at stake
    Odds of "13 million to one", give me a break!
Bingo or poker give some folks thrills
    Those meager winnings won't pay the bills
There's always Las Vegas, or Atlantic City too
    If you like real gambling, they're for you
It costs quite a bit to get yourself there
    The odds are you won't even win the plane fare
What's the answer?, I really don't know
    All I can say is: "Hard come, easy go!"

First class mail costs you more
    at least a nickel or a dime
But just like first class airplane seats
    it gets there at the same time

When the bank sends the monthly statement
    and my checking account's out of line
I decided very long ago
    to use their balance, not mine.

Each time the postman visits
    I'd like to run for the hills
But I can't delay, and still have to pay
    the mailbox full of new bills

Lawyers, lawyers everywhere
    to help me win a suit
Their fee leaves nothing left for me
    and they won the case, to boot.

Savings is a fine habit
    Like a squirrel or even a rabbit
But after all the taxes I gave
    there was nothing left for me to save

During my career, it was very clear
    as to which company paid your wages
The new tradition, is acquisition
    You'd better check the financial pages

While a frost may hurt the farm economy
    it works too fast, I fear
Why should we immediately pay more
    for crops which were picked last year

In April I'd be exultant
    if I were a Tax Consultant
They fill out your forms for a healthy price
    Who do they go to for their tax advice?

We struggled our way through college
    Worked hard to pay tuition back then
Now that we're successful alumni
    they expect us to start donating again

April brings springtime, in all its glory
    But something always ruins this story
It's hard to enjoy spring, and really relax
    working all night on my income tax

"Save it for a rainy day"
    you always hear the experts say
For me the time to spend is today
    Not when it's wet and you're too old to play

Penny poker at home is called illegal
    You may even be arrested and fined
But bet all that you own on State Lotteries
    and nobody seems to mind

Raising children is quite a feat
    Making sure they're healthy, with plenty to eat
They go off to college, your dreams are complete
    Then sit back and watch your savings deplete.

"No down payment", "Three years to pay"
    is the latest marketing trend
It may sound wonderful up front
    but the percentage gets you in the end.

Banks are failing everywhere
    Savings and Loans run for the hills
They tell me I'll now have more taxes to pay
    because I saved and paid my bills

If economizing is built into your genes
    stay away from Automatic Teller Machines
They can quickly satisfy all your cravings
    But they surely put a dent in your life savings!

Polite bank tellers act very funny
   They say "Thank you" when you withdraw money.

The winter is done, and spring has sprung
   Birds and flowers the season has brung
In April our clocks move ahead one hour
   Then, boom, April 15th turns it all sour!

Why do credit card companies
   (when your high balance has you crazed)
write a friendly letter saying:
   "Your credit limit has been raised"?

Money doesn't grow on trees
   That's a figment of your dreams
In reality, it grows in boxes
   called automatic teller machines.

A DAY
AT THE BEACH

TRIP TO THE BEACH

We retired to Sarasota, near Siesta Key
    Off season it is empty as can be
February and March we try to stay away
    All the snow birds are there to play

Grandchildren are here, so I took a chance
    Packed up the car, dressed in short pants
The picnic basket emptied the fridge
    We ate most of it while stuck at the bridge

The parking lot was full to the brim
    Chances for us appeared very dim
We circled and circled and circled around
    Hooray, a space was finally found

Off to the sand with all of our gear
    To find a spot where the view was clear
I looked around to see who was near
    There's no escaping rock music, I fear

Oh well, we might as well settle down
    Don't let the grandchildren see you frown
They came to enjoy the surf and sun
    On with the blockout, everyone

As we finally sat down, to take our ease
    I heard "Let's go swimming, Grandpa, please"
The very thought terrified me
    The Gulf temperature was sixty-three!

We swam and frolicked and ate our lunch
    Finally left for home in the traffic crunch
The car which I had carefully cleaned by hand
    Was completely filled with Siesta Beach sand

I love my family, every one
    I'm pleased they enjoyed the beach and sun
Without a doubt, they wore me out
    but everything we did, they raved about

Our peaceful house is peaceful no more
    But isn't that what a house is for?
The bedlam and noise didn't seem so bad
    after the double martini I had!

Short and tall, big and stout
    They flock to the beach and sit
Most I find, have a large behind
    and sitting's the best way to hide it.

———————

They drive, and drive, and drive, and drive
    To go south for some weeks in the sun.
When they arrive, for umbrellas they dive
    and constantly sit under one

———————

Bathing suits have really changed
    Perhaps I'm just losing my touch
You pay lots more, for a whole lot less
    and your skin it doesn't cover much.

———————

How do you tell a "snow bird"
    From we who are here all the year?
While we're still in bed, on the beach they turn red
    In spite of the lotion they smear.

———————

I watched children playing Hop-Scotch
    on our beach one day
Hopping looks like lots of fun
    But do Scotsmen play that way?

———————

As a weekend sailor I take exception
    and don't think it very funny
When they call a boat "a hole in the water
    you must constantly keep filled with money".

———————

Sharp shells cut your feet, seaweed mats your hair
    Sticky salt water creeps in everywhere
The sun broils your skin, each pore's full of sand
    Still we rush to the beach, ain't it grand!

We walk the beach together
    and smile as our muscles tone
Have you noticed the sad expression
    of those who must walk alone?

———————

A day at the beach I always find
    is a perfect way to really unwind
The girls in bikinis dazzle one's mind
    For them, Mother Nature has been very kind

———————

As I sit and watch the sailboats
    stretched out across the bay
It reminds me of Monday when I was young
    Sheets drying on laundry day

———————

Beach chairs are tricky gadgets
    They collapse when you try to recline
Their construction guarantees to give you
    a case of curvature of the spine.

———————

Skinny women on the beach wear bathing suit tops
    Fat and flabby men don't make this move
I sometimes think the reverse should be true
    and the scenery would greatly improve.

———————

Sand is found all over the world
    It is used to make concrete and glass
When you sit on the beach on a windy day
    sand fills every pore of your body.

———————

If I do nothing useful when at home
    I may feel guilty for days
That's why I like to lie on the beach
    You need no excuse to laze.

The sandpiper never seems to rest
    Digging sand for food, he tries his best
When a wave comes in, he runs like a jet
    I guess they don't like to get their feet wet.

What is a "T-Back" bathing suit?
    Well, I'll tell you loud and clear
In the front it's a brief bikini
    But you won't believe the view from the rear!

Oceans are widespread and deep
    and there's one secret that they keep
There's high tide and low tide, that I know
    But at low tide, where does all the water go?

Be they oversized or lengthy, bathing suits cannot hide
    all that extra weight you're carrying inside
Likewise, if you're too thin, there's not much to do
    Padding and stuffing won't disguise the real you
So, accept who you are, wear a comfortable bathing suit
    Forget your looks, real friends don't give a hoot!

I spent all day in the sun, lying on the sand motionless
    I suffered all next week, since I had been lotion-less!

"Fun in the sun", travel agents expound
    That's how their money is made
The sun is no bargain, and in the latest jargon
    It's much "cooler" in the shade.

Seagulls have thrived on many a shore
    for hundreds of years, and probably more
They roamed far and wide, independent and free
    eating clams and other food from the sea
Ain't it a shame, their old habits are dead
    They now flock to beaches and beg crumbs of bread.

A buxom blond was sunbathing one day
    on her stomach not wearing a top.
I was about to shout "Everybody up"
    but my wife convinced me to stop.

"Don't stay in the water too long"
    mothers on the beach always shout.
"Why can't you kids stop bugging me"
    they shout when they finally come out.

I looked at the overweight people lying all day
    on beach chairs in cabanas luxurious
I was tempted to tell them to get off their duffs
    But, no, it would just make them furious.

The crowd at the beach all looked up
    as a raincloud darkened the sky
then raced to their cars as fast as they could
    I suppose to keep their bathing suits dry.

The beach used to provide a peaceful day
    There was always plenty of room
Now this place has run out of space
    and they've added music boxes that boom!

Watching couples on the beach
    I've come to this conclusion
One or the other is always the boss
    thus eliminating marital confusion.

FAMILY CIRCLE

THE NEW GENERATION

It seems to me, that in olden times
    Whenever we heard those Holiday chimes
Grandma and grandpa would surely know
    That to their house the brood would go
But now it seems the rules have changed
    The children have it all arranged
"You're both retired, is that not true?"
    "Why should we have to visit you?"
"Pack your bags, prepare to flee"
    "We'll meet you at the airport at three"
"We love to have you here, you see"
    "But don't you dare shake the tree"
"You raised us once, with a firm hand"
    "But modern-day children you don't understand"
Their "new" approach has a familiar ring
    We told our parents the very same thing.
We bite our lips and nod and smile
    Both realizing all the while
There's nothing new under the sun
    and our children's problems have just begun
Wait until our grandchildren grow
    Our kids will find out how little they know.
One happy note to end this drama
    I can go home with grand-mama.

ANTICIPATION

Looking forward to the holidays
    is a time of Joy, in many ways
We'll get to see our far-flung kin
    many weeks before, our plans begin
Make plane reservations before it's too late
    It won't be long, we can hardly wait
The day finally comes, Thanksgiving is here
    Hugs and kisses greet all near and dear
Our children are adults, long on their own
    It's hard to believe how the grandchildren have grown
In spite of that, we have our dreams
    that nothing has changed, how silly that seems
It doesn't take long, to our dismay
    to realize that life doesn't work that way
Each family is different, they lead their own life
    They're children no more, they're now husband and wife
No matter how much we'd like time to go slow
    on their separate paths our children must go
We'll still meet each year on Thanksgiving day
    but there's something I must reluctantly say
No matter how much you enjoy meeting on vacation
    It's never as good as the anticipation!

Children are a gift from heaven
    Grandchildren are even more so
Since most everyone else has them too
    our bragging must really bore so

"You must go to college, to gain some knowledge"
    I advised my son with conviction
"Even if you fail, and come home dragging your tail,
    it might still improve your diction"

We two started off with a few children
    Then grandchildren to make us proud
Add son-in-laws, in-laws, and others
    The next thing we knew, we're a crowd!

Here comes another birthday
    with cards, and gifts, and song
Why doesn't my loving family
    treat me that way all year long?

A good marriage is like a great symphony
    If yours isn't, you have my sympathy

We always liked to play our part
    and filled our home with modern art
Our tastes in art now have a new call
    The grandchildren's photos cover each wall

I often wonder how nice it would
    if only my children had listened to me
On the other hand, for goodness sakes
    They would have made the same mistakes

Our granddaughter has just turned seventeen
    In our eyes, she's a beauty queen
Like all teenagers, her priorities are strange
    Not so long ago her priority was a diaper change

First a spouse, then a house
    A mortgage, then children, and a pet
Life always starts off so simply
    But, oh, how complicated it will get!

When youngsters first learn how to walk
    (It usually happens before they can talk)
They lurch, and fall, and stumble, and flop
    But, oh, how they sleep when they finally stop.

Prizefighting is like a bad marriage
    They punch and jab until they're sore
No matter how many times they are beaten
    they insist on coming back for more

Why does my three year old grandson still refuse
    to try to learn to tie his shoes?
He's smarter than most of us, by far
    when it comes to working the VCR

The alphabet, from A to Z
    is memorized by children before they are three
Don't credit the parents for this amazing feat
    We owe it all to Sesame Street.

My Grandchildren watch MTV
    Their taste in music has been lowered
I watched with them one day and thought
    The TV was stuck on "fast forward"

Family photos tend to collect
    on the desk, in drawers, or the wall
We finally put them all in albums
    and now we never see them at all!

When we were kids we bought chewing gum
    The free baseball cards were just a "ho-hum"
If only we'd known as we threw them away
    that they would be worth a fortune today.

You will never win an argument with your wife
    if you're stubborn and take the wrong tack
Before the fight, admit she's right
    That should get her off your back.

Teenagers can be a tribulation and a trial
    For your guidance they don't give a hoot
Through it all, it helps to recall
    that as infants, they were so cute.

At their home, my grandchildren have every known toy
    yet they often get bored and wail.
But on the beach, they can play for hours
    with some sand, a shovel, and a pail.

––––––––––

If you remember your wedding anniversary
    you are much smarter than I'm
My poor memory doesn't phase my wife
    She reminds me in plenty of time.

––––––––––

Wouldn't it be nice, if we could try things twice
    to correct the mistakes that we make
It could help you steer to a more successful career
    but one wife is all I can take!

POTPOURRI

I HATE TO COMPLAIN, BUT

It's time for me to loudly shout:

"Here are some things I can do without"
    Music TV and broccoli
    Fast foods and ugly moods
    French cooks and comic books
    Smog in L.A and Father's Day
    Traffic lights and foggy nights
    Head waiters and alligators
    Woolen socks and chicken pox
    Garden weeds and sesame seeds
    Dentist's drills and diet pills
    Tight shoes and club dues
    Punk rock and vapor lock
    Long hair and ready-to-wear
    Designated hitters and flagpole sitters
    Auto mechanics and stock market panics
    Tight pants and fire ants
    Paper plates and blind dates
    Dirty glasses and exhaust gases
    Gift shops and traffic cops
    Head lice and my golf slice
    Ice cold showers and artificial flowers
    Smelly cigars and antique cars
    Noisy pets and string quartets
    Household chores and party bores
    Income tax and ear wax
    Alarm clocks and young jocks
    Morning jogs and barking dogs
    Cowboy boots and turkey shoots
    A long sermon and PeeWee Herman
    Head colds and Jello molds
    Modern art and jump start
    Exercise machines and canned sardines

    It's getting to be quite a bore
    Every day I uncover more

"DO AS I SAY"

Everyone has the future to face
    whether your past was worthwhile or a disgrace
Tomorrow is coming, without any doubt
    It's time to wash your dirty linen out
If you won't do that, I'm sorry to say
    You'll never get out of your rut, called "today"
Make your move, be a go-getter
    Your life may not change, but you'll feel a lot better
As for me, after much self-reflection
    I decided you cannot improve on perfection
I'm not very modest, as you can easily see
    since my advice never applies to me!

IT'S A PUZZLEMENT

Crossword puzzles always used to be
    simple enough for people like me
Today they publish all sorts of new
    innovations to puzzles impossible to do
Some are called "Diagram-less", that gives me a laugh
    You're expected to solve it and draw your own graph
"Cryptic" crosswords will boggle your mind
    You have to be psychic, the answers to find
Then there are "Anacrostics" to face
    It takes a genius to fill every space
I'd sure like to use a battering ram
    on whoever invented the "Cryptogram"
Your mind has to be somewhat twisted
    if attempting a "Logic" puzzle you have persisted
Crosswords used to provide relaxation and rest
    They've turned into a college entrance test!

IN-SECURITY

Now that I have reached that stage called maturity
    where is that elusive goal called security?
You are never secure from storms: snow or rain
    and even less from worry, aches or pain
Gilt-edged securities are a laugh
    They slide right down the economic graph
Income's not sound, prices skyward bound
    How do you get off this merry-go-round?
The most logical answer that I can find
    is that true security is a frame of mind.

The "studio audience" is a crowd of folks
    who have nothing better to do
Why do they applaud and laugh so long
    when it's not at all funny to you?

Staples are very helpful to some
    to attach papers in the mails
They have another side effect
    Removing them breaks fingernails

I have my own movie ratings
    "PG" means plenty of gore
"R" stands for simply revolting
    "G" they don't make anymore!

I pass the beauty parlor
    when I go downtown to dine
The ladies sitting under all those hoods
    look like a science fiction assembly line

Doctors, for very good reasons
    carry "beepers" wherever they go
I sometimes think all those other folks
    are wearing them just for "show"

A sofa is a fancy seat
   with no place to rest your head
The type of couch I really prefer
   is the one that converts to a bed

_____

"A friend in need is a friend indeed"
   That adage is not very clear
I seem to find, when I'm in a financial bind
   that most of my "friends" disappear.

_____

The New York Times on Sunday
   is almost too heavy to lift
One comment about their crossword
   To solve it takes quite a gift

_____

I sit in my barber's emporium
   As he cuts, I think it's not fair
that the people who aren't going bald
   are the ones who don't cut their hair

_____

Weather forecasts fill the air
   Spring, summer, winter, and fall
They're very long, and often wrong
   I'll stick to my crystal ball

_____

Foreign operas are so confusing
   Appreciation for them I never had
The singers probably don't understand it either
   That's why they always look mad

_____

I tried to play the piano
   "No use", my teacher objected
"You don't use both hands correctly"
   It seems mine are not well-connected.

Symphony concerts go on for hours
    Between each movement there is a pause
The only way I know it has ended
    is when I hear the applause

Don't ever repeat your old mistakes
    is an adage that's not a mystery
If you think of all the wars we've had
    We "ain't" learned a thing from history.

Some women's hair is two feet high
    Like it was styled with an egg beater
I always seem to sit behind
    someone like that in the theater

I find it hard to be discreet
    when a bigot I happen to meet
After he goes down in defeat
    his departure makes my day complete

I love the circus with all its thrills
    and clowns with their funny lids
Lions who are tame, men who eat flames
    Who said it's just for kids?

I only use two fingers
    to type at a pretty fast pace
The other fingers come into action
    when I use both hands to erase

I'm a very honest person
    and never break laws, I hope
Why when I leave a motel
    do I "steal" the shampoo and soap?

The major networks are always warring
  and fill the air with shows that are boring
I trust, like me, that you're still waiting
  for a few good programs, despite their ratings

Water conservation is urgently needed
  Levels of water tables have seriously receded
We're good at wasting water, yet most people think
  they don't want "recycled" water in their sink
To solve this dilemma, a name change is in order
  Instead of "treated sewage", call it "treated water"

Star light, star bright
  Too many stars I've seen tonight
I wish I may, I wish I might
  get to sleep before it's light

We recycle newsprint, cans, plastic, and glass
  None of these to the trash will we pass
But all of these efforts will surely fall
  unless we eliminate all that junk mail!

Why do women, usually so calm and clerical
  in an electrical storm get so hysterical?

Of all the stories I've been told
  ethnic humor leaves me cold
Put all those insults on the shelf
  Try telling jokes about yourself

I wish I could understand why
  Most authors wait for public figures to die
before they let the scandals fly
  I guess time passing makes it legal to lie

Chomping popcorn, slurping coke
    Ice cream from Dairy Queen
Movie theaters have become
    restaurants with a screen

"T" shirts used to be worn
    underneath to keep you warm
Now they advertise beer and sex
    Instead of "T", they should be rated "X"

Life can be like a ceiling fan
    as it circles but gets nowhere
If we don't get off our duff and escape
    we'll be trapped just blowing hot air

For "heartburn" there are pills by the score
    "Headache" remedies fill every drug store
"Headburn" is prevented with lotion or a hat
    but "heartache", I know no medicine for that

If you want to see how you really look
    check that photo in your passport book

Everyone's hiring consultants these days
    If you don't know your job, I guess it pays.
The consultants, themselves, are overjoyed
    They earn much more than when they were employed.

In summer, thunderstorms arrive most every night
    Some are so violent, they give folks a fright.
Bright bolts of lightning, then a loud thunder clap
    It looks like they're searching for someone to zap.

Through High School and College, I found it rough
    learning Algebra, Geometry, Calculus and all that stuff
If you think those days were thoroughly confused
    Looking back, I find that none of it was used!

I am called an artistic illiterate
    Modern art, I can't seem to figure-it
If the painters would be more specific
    I might become less hypocritic.

We all seem enthralled with trivia
    Like: "What's the population of Namibia?"
As we battle with Trivial Pursuit
    at most answers I'm completely mute.

Jack was nimble, Jack was quick
    He stole my silver and a candlestick
Jack soon discovered that crime won't win
    The silver was plate, and the candlestick tin!

If you can't seem to fall asleep
    don't waste time counting sheep
My system hasn't failed me yet
    I just turn on the TV set

Riding the New York subway on a crowded day
    the passengers are quite a sight, I dare to say
Tattoos, earrings, and outlandish clothes
    I sat next to a boy with a ring through his nose.
Painted faces and fingernails in every bright shade
    Weird looking hair styles were all on parade.
"T" shirts with messages very obscene
    Sneakers in colors of bright pink or green.
Some looked like they had just come in out of the rain
    Who said the graffiti is all outside the train?

Some folks watch their calories
    Others think it's pure nonsense
Take everything you crave, but eat very fast
    and it will seem to ease your conscience.

————————

It's hard to express, how much I detest
    a "wrong number" call when I've laid down to rest

————————

It's a privilege to be, in a country that's free
    Free to complain, but don't try it on me!

————————

Did you ever watch people caught in the rain?
    Running madly for cover, with a look of great pain
If you've got an umbrella, why not employ it?
    If not you'll get wet, relax and enjoy it

————————

These days when boys to the prom do go
    They're dressed like the comics in a vaudeville show

————————

Sometimes I get the feeling when people stare
    I'm in the minority 'cause I shave and cut my hair

————————

Lightning is spectacular to watch
    You may glory at nature's wonder
But don't stand outdoors watching it flash
    if it's followed too closely by thunder

————————

They say good music can calm the savage breast
    if the melody and lyrics are pleasantly expressed
Most people consider "pop" music absurd
    Maybe because they can't understand a word!

————————

I use the same barber, year after year
    He does the job, both front and rear
Why hold up a mirror to view my coif?
    It's too late then if he took too much off

We've gone for a long time without any rain
    Now it's pouring, we gripe and complain
We don't like drought, but we want sunny days
    Believe me friend, "You can't have it both ways!"

I'm a long time subscriber to many magazines
    and I don't mean to sound glib or surly
but they must be awfully short of cash
    when renewal invoices arrive six months early

The county dump is filled each day by gardeners
    with truckloads of freshly cut grass
Cattle and horses would love that stuff
    but past them the trucks always pass

It's hard to be funny and still make sense
    I'll give you a laugh at my expense
Whenever I try to be really serious
    everyone smiles, it's very mysterious

If your car repair doesn't take, the mechanic makes good
    The new TV failed, they did what they could
The furniture got scratched, they repaired the wood
    You don't pay, till it does what it should.
But go to the doctor to cure your ills
    He quickly prescribes expensive potions or pills
And, by the way, you must pay in advance
    instead of giving the medicine a chance.

If you've never had a martini that's dry
   try it at home where your bed is nearby

Here's how to tell when you've had enough
   Your talking's not smooth, and your walking is rough

"Friends, Romans, countrymen" I set no store on
   It's a perfect example of a double oxymoron.

It doesn't seem fair, to see all that hair
   on beards, rather than on heads that are bare.

Our telephone answerer has a big plus
   Telemarketing salespeople hang up on us.

I've given up the beach for my quiet patio
   Those loud radios were driving me batty-o

I've heard of a job that would suit me just fine
   A vintner is seeking a taster of wine.

Modern bathing suits are like a supermarket magazine
   They expose things that few have ever seen.

Airline discounts sound like very good deals
   What kills your budget are the hotels and meals.

"Come Fly With Me", Frank likes to sing
   but he'll never replace Bing or Nat King.

How do you explain to teenage daughter
   not to do as we did, but as we taught 'er

Buffalo chicken wings are hot, all right
    and they continue to burn throughout the night.

———————

"Don't go near the water" may be helpful advice
    and it sure is helpful over scotch and ice.

———————

Wouldn't it be nice, as we turn out the light
    if we also could turn off our brain for the night?

———————

No matter what time our mailman delivers
    the arrival of bills gives me the shivers.

———————

After every crisis, political or crimes gory
    every columnist claims the inside story

———————

Fast food restaurants can put on weight
    if you digest it as quickly as you ate

———————

If anyone doubts that the Earth is round
    let them sit down on solid ground
and stare out to sea, keeping their eyes on
    ships as they come up from beyond the horizon.

———————

Secrets in writing may get you in dutch
    with the I.R.S., wives, accountants and such
If you really must expose yourself in a letter
    the best place to file it is in the office shredder

———————

Travel allows you to re-discover the past
    but you must pay the fare and hotel deposit
It's much cheaper to explore, you'll find history galore
    just visiting your attic and spare closet.

Long hair hangs down their rear
    Fancy earrings are displayed in each ear
With all that jewelry and lengthy curls
    How do you tell the boys from the girls?

Clouds appear so light and fluffy
    as they float suspended in air
If the rain they contain weighs so much
    what in the world keeps them up there?

We went to a Shakespeare festival
    featuring swashbucklers and villains to dread
It was all very serious and impressive
    but I didn't understand a word that was said.

Life is like a game of "Trivial Pursuit"
    A really good memory can often bear fruit
I wonder, at times, whether important old realities
    have somehow been converted into trivialities.

INDEPENDENCE DAY

On the Fourth of July we watched our parade
    What a wonderful sound the marching bands made
Soldiers and sailors all strode with great pride
    Isn't it grand, they're all on our side?

Then came the local groups en masse
    Boy Scouts, Girl Scouts, the gymnastics class
The politicians all rode, at marching they balk
    They're out of condition, except when they talk

Veterans of our wars were driven in floats
    That's when we felt the lumps in our throats
It's not wars we honor with all this to-do
    but peace, and the brave ones who made it come true

The parade is gone, the fireworks are done
    The ballgame is over, and our school won
Back to work, all holidays must end
    But this one is special to me, my friend

IT'S EXHAUSTING

Although we really hadn't ought-er
    we waste an awful lot of water
Civilization is on the brink
    of not having enough to drink
One of the big abuses, by far
    is constantly washing your car
To me, there's no sweat or strain
    letting nature wash it with rain
Lawn sprinkling is another crime
    Must grass be green all the time?
Believe me, you won't ever smell sour
    if you spend less time taking a shower
To further conserve water, I propose
    Stop washing the driveway with your hose
There are countless other ways, of course
    to stop the loss of this resource
Nature took care of the plants and grasses
    long before man invented drinking glasses
So drink all the water you choose
    and even pour some in your booze
But stop all the other wasteful uses
    or nobody wins, and mankind loses.